THE WORLD MATTERS

THE WORLD MATTERS

An Insight Into The World's Burning Issues

Kavin S. Kanagasabai

iUniverse, Inc.
New York Lincoln Shanghai

The World Matters

An Insight Into The World's Burning Issues

iUniverse books may be ordered through booksellers or by contacting:

iUniverse
2021 Pine Lake Road, Suite 100
Lincoln, NE 68512
www.iuniverse.com
1-800-Authors (1-800-288-4677)

Because of the dynamic nature of the Internet, any Web addresses or links contained in this book may have changed since publication and may no longer be valid.

The views expressed in this work are solely those of the author and do not necessarily reflect the views of the publisher, and the publisher hereby disclaims any responsibility for them.

ISBN: 978-0-595-44341-3 (pbk)
ISBN: 978-0-595-88671-5 (ebk)

Printed in the United States of America

To my parents
With deepest love and gratitude

CONTENTS

Preface

The present time is one in which the dominant mindset is a feeling of obscure perplexity. At the nascent stage of the 21st century, humanity is still at loggerheads in resolving important issues affecting it. The world, as it integrated closer through technological progress, has also suffered many a wedge through ideological differences among nations over issues affecting them.

The world has continually managed to throw up new challenges and unusual difficulties, yet the responses to tackling such issues remain ambiguous at best and confrontational at worst. This condition presents an intellectual challenge as the world, despite being aware of the difficulties that it is facing, still has not managed to be consensual in resolving globally important matters despite its ever-shrinking geographical distances.

The interactions between nations, organisations, and peoples in the world have undergone a sea change from being relatively aloof and distant a few decades ago to something more intimate and affectedly closer. The movement of people, money, labour, ideas, and ideologies and the pace with which businesses and markets have broken many barriers, which were once seen as insurmountable, have now been taken for granted thanks to technological advances in travel and communications. As countries have become increasingly interdependent on one another even as they are solely and largely responsible for managing their internal affairs, there are issues, which they cannot solve just by themselves but only through mutual understanding and global co-operation.

Not many issues afflicting and affecting countries could easily be brushed aside as solely belonging to rich countries or poor countries, to developed ones or developing ones or, for that matter, to those in the West or those in the East. Issues such as poverty, disease and debt are widely associated with poor countries, not to mention socio-political instability in unstable regimes. Unemployment, immigration, terrorism and environment occupy, perhaps more than any other issue, the political agenda of rich countries. However, these issues can no longer be scrutinized in isolation nor can they be resolved without involving governments in both rich and poor countries. The intensification of globalization, or in other words, a rapidly globalizing world, has not only blurred the geographical divide between nations but it has also moulded the nature of problems from being merely 'local' to becoming 'global' thus continually fashioning change in an ever-spiralling Hegelian dialectical mode.

Some of the global changes today present the world with a set of issues demanding urgent attention. The role of market economy, the contribution of international trade and industrialization of developing countries to pollution, the stark reality of depleting non-renewable energy resources, the abuse of human rights, the urge for freedom and the political agenda of exporting democracy into countries where human freedom is still viewed with a 'jaundiced' eye and such matters today engage world governments, international bodies, activists, politicians, writers, anarchists and the lay person in debates and arguments. Besides the vulnerability of international peace and the seemingly endless war over geo-political or religious interests further pose an indefinite challenge to global stability.

The cardinal purpose of this book, 'The World Matters' is to highlight the five major issues—capitalism, democracy, environment, terrorism and human rights—the world is grappling with today in varying degrees. This book is meant for academicians, students, leaders, policy makers, scholars and for anyone interested in politics, social issues, public policy, humanities and importantly, the much-debated issue of globalization.

Capitalism—widely branded as 'global capitalism' because of its global reach and its impact on international governments through open markets crisscrossing geographical boundaries—is often railed for its global dimension. The detractors of capitalism often see it as a means of exploitation of both people and natural resources to satiate man's selfish ends. I have taken the view and argued that capitalism has, by far, been the more humane and more prosperous of all the economic models, or systems experimented by man. 'The Importance of Capitalism' is the first essay in this book. In the essay, I underline its role in bringing prosperity to hundreds of millions of people whose lives, previously, had been bound at the altar of heart-wrenching poverty. I have also dug into the histories of some countries' economic status before they switched from communism/socialism/authoritarianism to capitalism. The essay on capitalism argues how important it is for governments to make use of a system (capitalism) that clearly has proven, over the years, to be better than any of its alternatives such as communism or socialism. I also discuss in the essay on how capitalism is prevented from serving its purpose by vested interests in both rich and poor country governments as they promote their own narrow agenda. While poor countries show reluctance in lifting some of the regulations, red tape and barriers to let capitalism, or open markets, work to their benefit, rich countries inadvertently undermine capitalism, for instance, by not scrapping costly subsidies on which their less productive farmers are fed through the taxpayers' money.

In 'The Appeal of Democracy', I stress the fact that democracy, to this day, remains the more popular form of government than any type of authoritarian system yet it remains vulnerable to military subversion and coups. Nonetheless, democracy has grown from strength to strength in its journey to where it is today. Due to its popular appeal, the veil of democracy is often used by brutal regimes to cover up political atrocities. The government of Robert Mugabe in Zimbabwe, for instance, presides over a sham democracy by conducting farce elections to legitimize its rule of political intimidation. I further underline the fact that mere holding of elections does not constitute democracy if it does not fulfil other democratic requirements such as freedom of opposition, media, independent judiciary, and free association of public. I also argue about the lopsided philosophizing of the so-called 'Asian Values'—often cited as an anomaly with democracy. Besides, I bring to the reader's attention the link between 'economic well-being' and 'democracy', and the standing of Islam in the realm of democracy.

In 'The Spectre of Terror', I focus on the struggle of Islam and its distorted survival at a time when it remains hijacked by its fanatic followers, hardened fundamentalists, and unrelenting extremists. I also contend the popular view that poverty contributes to terrorism. In addition, I further analyze the so-called America's pursuit of 'war on terror' and offer reasons as to why such 'limited' strategy can never be adequate to subjugate terrorism.

In the essay, 'The pertinence of Human Rights', I endeavour to point to the abuse of human rights by those countries, such as America and Britain, long considered bastions of human rights, and their disregard for individual rights as their governments are intent on pursuing their own political agenda. I further throw some light upon the authoritarian regimes of Cuba, North Korea and alike where human rights grab the least of attention in their political administration. Despite making human slavery and the international condemnation of such despicable practices, slavery of fellow human beings is still prevalent in many parts of the world. I have also focused on the problem of 'child labour' in India for the singular reason that India has the unenviable record of having the highest number of child workers in the world.

In the final essay, 'The complexity of Environment', I consider the various aspects of the environment—from air and water pollution harming the environment, to the availability of non-renewable resources, to the importance of the growth of economy particularly in developing countries, and to the very serious issue of global warming. The environmental conundrum is, perhaps, the most engaging debate taking place around the world today. I conclude this essay with the argument that both 'ecology' and 'economy' are complementary provided compromises are made on either side of the sect rather than clamouring for the blind negligence, or outright scrapping of one for the sake of the other.

In short, this book talks about different issues, considered the most important and most exigent which assume a sweeping global dimension. The aim of this book is to bring to the reader the facts and realities that often get buried in popular rhetoric while at the same time making the reader look at the different dimensions of the issues discussed in the book.

This book is the culmination of my research and my own analysis over two years. During my student days in the University, I talked about numerous topical issues, in several seminars and symposia, and often felt an intense need to put forth my ideas for the benefit of the general reader.

I would like to take this opportunity to thank Dr K L Madhavan, my professor at Pachaiyappa's College, University of Madras, India, for inspiring my outlook to wider social issues. He had largely been instrumental, during my time at the College, for my participation in countless seminars, youth exchange programmes, social welfare activities, debates and several literary events. I owe a great debt to Derek Reece, my editor from Authors On Line. His careful and studious examination of my writing, and his comments and suggestions have improved the lucidity of the contents in this book.

I must also express my gratitude to my parents-in-law, Ermano and Marina Frate for their support while I had worked on this book. Last, but not least, I would like to thank my wife Federica for her support, motivation and patience right from the beginning to the completion of this book.

CHAPTER 1

▼

THE IMPORTANCE OF CAPITALISM

We live in a world of slogans and mantras. They vie incessantly to occupy the realms of 'fact' and 'reality'. Just as a piece of iron gets rusty and loses its original impression after it has long been in exposure, words like 'fact' and 'reality' too become effaced at the gaze of sloganeering and mantra-chanting cynics. Fact and reality represent different things to different people. There is the type of 'fact' that expresses itself with promise and the type of 'reality' that presents itself with hope.

There is also the other type of 'twisted fact' that sabotages promise and of 'blinkered reality' that undermines hope. These ideas are quite popular among the cavillers of capitalism in that they constantly envisage social disintegration when, in fact and in reality, capitalism has facilitated an unprecedented furtherance of prosperity. This furtherance of prosperity has lifted hundreds of millions of suffering men, women, and children out of flagitious poverty.

The economic freedom ushered in by capitalism to the world's numerous poor has given them wealth; a new social status that had hitherto remained the privilege of their higher social echelons; and, a feeling of liberty that had long been suppressed under the iron fist of repression. Yet, the tendency to undermine capitalism from its roots is still running strong among a cross-section of individuals. The sabotage of promise and the undermining of hope thrive on the exaggeration of events and intimidation of ordinary people through panic. Capitalism is likened to a machine that runs over open terrains ignoring familiar boundaries as it exhilarates and frightens. As it goes, the machine throws off enormous mows of wealth and bounty while it leaves behind great furrows of wreckage.[1]

True, there are furrows of wreckage scattered around the world today. To assert that the wreckages are products of capitalism is to perceive, either ignorantly or deliberately, both 'fact' and 'reality' with a jaundiced vision and twist them with a malevolent intent. Any wreckage that is left around us today is, in fact, the remainder of an 'aggregate' accumulated largely owing to economic bondage that slid billions of people into heart-wrenching poverty and misery. Much of the wreckage, though, has now been narrowed and slimmed greatly.

Overall, life is getting better. Globally, the life expectancy of people has vastly increased; infant mortality markedly curtailed; world poverty considerably snipped; and food supply profusely boosted. The world is not perfect. It never will be. It will probably be perfect in a utopian dream but not in the real world manned by imperfect beings. All that mankind can do is to realize that it can only strive honestly and industriously to make things get better—continually and perpetually.

Capitalism, because of its inherent ability to change and be changed, has, all along its chequered history but successful march, managed to whittle down its shortcomings promptly. It came through unrelenting attacks from anarchists; socialists; communists whose ideals have made not even half the inroad, as capitalism has made, into the lives of people apart from piecemeal protestations from time to time. The challenge before us is not to find that 'elusive' perfect system. The challenge lies in our willingness to keep improving imperfect things as we move along with the rest of our global fellow beings.

Catalyst for prosperity

The Malthusian fear that the world would run out of food, thereby plunging the whole of humanity into an unimaginable crisis, due to the geometrical growth (2, 4, 8, 16 and so on) of population and as a consequence of arithmetical production (2, 4, 6, 8 and so on) of food, still attracting an exclamatory expression, was proved categorically incorrect by human inventiveness—for instance, the break-

---

1. William Greider, *One World, Ready or Not*, (New York, Simon & Schuster, 1997), p. 11

through of Green revolution. The world found its first solid expression in the exuberant optimism of human ingenuity.

In the 1960s, the Green Revolution increased food production through better technology, stemming from the improved strains of wheat, rice, maize, and other cereals. Countries that suffered from shrinking food production such as India, Pakistan, Philippines, Mexico, Sri Lanka, and a number of other underdeveloped countries during the 60s profoundly benefited from it. Between 1961 and 1999, the average daily food supply per person increased 24 percent globally. In developing countries, it rose by 39 percent, to 2,684 calories. By 1999, China's average daily food supply had gone up 82 percent, to 3,044 calories, from a barely subsistence level of 1,636 calories in 1950–1.[2]

The increase in global food supply, it must be noted, has occurred in the face of expeditious rise in global population. The Food and Agriculture Organization (FAO), in its report on World Agriculture: towards 2015/2030[3] reckons that population growth will be growing at an average of 1.1 percent a year up to 2030, compared to 1.7 percent annually over the past 30 years. The growth in world demand for agricultural products is expected to slow further from an average of 2.2 percent annually over the past 30 years to 1.5 percent per year until 2030. In developing countries, the slowdown will be more dramatic, from 3.7 percent for the past 30 years to an average of 2 percent until 2030. It is heartening to know that the world population will be increasingly well-fed by 2030, with 3,050 kilocalories (kcal). That is a sharp increase from 2,360 kcal per person per day in the mid-1960s, the decade that marked Green Revolution, to 2,800 kcal today. The most reassuring forecast, by the FAO, is the decline in the number of hungry people in developing countries from 777 million today to about 440 million in 2030.

The misplaced argument that the world's poor are impoverished to the point of barrenness by the rise of global capitalism is veritably a medley of 'twisted fact' and 'blinkered reality'. It is 'twisted fact' because it fails to argue with facts and figures. It is 'blinkered reality' because it plainly fails to see the broad transformation of the lives of the poor for better across the world. When pessimism pervades, even promising signs get trampled under the heavy strain of scepticism. Is it a consequence of the rich countries of the world sucking the resources out of

---

2. Martin Wolf, *Why Globalisation Works*, (New Haven and London, Yale NB, 2005) p. 165
3. Food and Agriculture Organization, *World Agriculture: towards 2015/2030*, Summary Report, 2002

poverty-stricken countries? The answer is, "not really so". And the answer is not easy to explain either. Twenty four countries, according to the World Bank report which terms them as new 'globalisers', as varied as China, India, Hungary, Vietnam and Bangladesh have seen an enormous decline in their poverty rates. They have, at the same time, seen their income levels soar manifestly. Their economic growth has been spectacular. In fact, these countries recorded economic growth twice as much as rich countries.

A report by the World Bank, "Globalization, growth and poverty", argues that there have been both winners as well as losers in an increasingly integrated and integrating world. Living standards in many countries have improved enormously. Poverty has cascaded to a great low. There are three groups that have been affected by globalization. Firstly, nothing much has happened in the rich countries apart from the fact that they got richer in the midst of plenty. Secondly, developing countries that have integrated themselves in a global economy, with a combined population of about 3 billion have made extraordinary strides in their living standards growing at 5 percent during the 1990s as against 2 percent for the rich countries. Thirdly, it is a worry that many poor countries with about 2 billion people, of which about 1.2 billion live on less than $1 per day, have been marginalized from the benefits of globalization often with declining incomes and rising poverty. More than 40 percent of those 1.2 billion are in South Asia—that is, India, Bangladesh, Pakistan and Sri Lanka; 23 percent are in East Asia including China.[4]

It is not just that the markets are not working for them but a number of other influences keep them and their societies crippled from making any significant progress. Excess protection of non-performing companies, subsidies to inefficient and unproductive entities, communal violence, political corruption, populism and instability, absence of democracy and stifling of freedom of the media, creaking infrastructure and environmental degradation, keep rearing their ugly heads, frequently in some places and continually in other places. But wherever capitalism has taken roots, it bears fruits, remarkably and strikingly, for the societies cutting across lines of races, nationalities and borders.

No more begging bowl

Once known as Annam. Now it is called Vietnam. Annam was the name given by China when it seized Vietnam around 111 BC. Later, in the 19th century, the

---

4. Bill Emmott, *20:21 Vision, The Lessons of the 20th Century for the 21st*, (London, Penguin, 2004), p. 221

French took control of Vietnam. During the Second World War, Japan conquered it and established a government under state Emperor Bao Dai. After the war, Bao Dai government collapsed as the nationalist liberation movement Viet Minh took over under its leader, Ho Chi Minh. That promptly worried the French who tried to reassert their control on Vietnam but the French were defeated in the war by the Viet Minh. In 1954, the country divided. The Northern part fell under the communist thumb of Ho Chi Minh. The Southern region fell under the French which also had its legitimacy recognized by many western countries including the United States, as it became increasingly involved in Vietnamese politics.

Fearful of the spread of communism and the collapse of South Vietnam against the powerful North, the US ran into a bloody conflict, in 1965, with the North. America deployed thousands of its troops in Vietnam. It rained bombs. The war turned infernal. Thousands of lives were lost. The awfully bloody war extended for years until it was finally called off in a treaty in Paris in 1973 when the outcome of the war turned out politically disastrous for America due to vehement public outcry at home, economic mishap and the loss of thousands of its soldiers. The US withdrew its troops as well as its support for South Vietnam. In a way, it let down the South Vietnamese. The war cost Vietnam, and badly. In 1975, after the US troops vacated Vietnam, Ho Chi Minh's nationalist forces overran the South forcing it to surrender to the North. Vietnam once again reunited. Vietnam became a socialist republic in 1976 with the vision of the country's leadership deeply rooted in the ideals of communism.

Finally Vietnam emerged out of the spoilages of war but not from the misfortune that was to follow. The country lost its financial aid from the former Soviet Bloc as it could no longer aid its ideological ally because it had already showered a lot of its money on the nationalist government during the war against America. Vietnam grew obsessed with its centrally-planned economy. It became internationally remote and its economy began to deteriorate quickly.

The virtues of market economy did not dawn on the country's leadership until Vietnam, in the year of 1985, slipped into a grave economic crisis. Its productivity fell. Vietnam's economic plans and policies failed to bear fruit with dramatic trends between 1976 and the watershed year, 1986, during which time the country's economy was affected by instability with a chunky budget deficit, dwindling agricultural production, and a ballooning foreign debt. It had to depend on imports to meet the country's demand of basic goods. The country's economic situation was so dire that it had to import "… 1.5 million tonnes of rice and 60 million meters of cloth and there were signs of instability with a large budget deficit and growing foreign debt in both convertible and non-convertible currencies (reaching 8.5 billion (Russian) roubles and $US 1.5 billion)."[5] The level of prices went out of control as Vietnam's inflation rate sky-rocketed to a staggering 775 percent! In 1986, the government abandoned its Marxist-driven policies in favour of a market economy by introducing a package of economic reforms which it called *Doi Moi*, or renovation. . It was during the landmark year of 1986 that the country overhauled its economic policies and Vietnam entered the world of liberal economy. Its economic gates were opened to the world. For the first time, perhaps in its entire history, the face of Vietnam was to undergo fundamental change

The introduction of *Doi Moi* saw a series of reform measures: the nescient government policies instrumental in the strangulation of the economy was shunned; the State Owned Enterprises (SOEs) were given autonomy and the subsidies they had heretofore enjoyed were terminated; the SOEs were now obliged to obtain bank loans, pay interest as well as taxes. The banking system was reorganized and the private sector was encouraged to embark upon a rigorous commercial activity. Exports were encouraged by a reduced reliance on quotas and the issue of licenses for export activity passed to the local government rather than being controlled by central authorities.[6]

In short, governmental spoon-feeding and pampering of the communist era gave way to an enterprising market economy. The first five *Doi Moi* years (1986–1990) led to heady economic pay-offs. Vietnam's paddy cultivation expanded from 18 million tonnes per year to 21.5 million tonnes, shifting from importing rice to exporting rice. Vietnam became the third largest rice exporter in the world. Industrial production of electricity, steel, and cement increased. Crude oil output rose from 40,000 tonnes (1986) to 2.7 million tonnes (1990). The annual average increase in exports was 28 percent.[7]

The country's inflation fell from a spectacularly unmanageable 775 percent in 1986 to 67.5 percent in 1991, and then to an impressively manageable 5 percent in 1997. Vietnam improved its economic performance even when its population boomed from about 50 million in 1976 to 66 million in 1990. In 2005 its popu-

---

5. Tran Vo Hung Son and Chau Van Thanh, *Analysis of the sources of economic growth of Viet Nam, Centre for International Management and Development Antwerp*, CAS (Centre for ASEAN Studies) Discussion Paper No 21, December 1998

6. ibid

7. ibid

lation reached 85 million while registering a splendid GDP growth rate of 7.5 percent. Vietnam's economic recovery did not come about by miracle but through a series of market-oriented sustained efforts underpinned by economic freedom. All along its open-market approach it managed to reduce the number of its poor.

As recently as 1993, the World Bank considered 58% of the population poor.[8] In the course of eleven years amidst growing population the poverty rate had dropped to "… 19.4 percent in 2004. Various social indicators, such as education levels and infant mortality, have also improved, reflected in an increase in the country's ranking in the United Nations Development Programme's human development index."[9] It had also come out of the Asian financial crisis by maintaining its growth rate around 4.8 percent. Small businesses were given a fillip by the Vietnamese government passing a new law in 2000 making initial set-up easier. By the end of 2002, more than 50,000 new firms sprouted vibrantly, making a vital contribution to the Vietnamese economy. Not all may be great in Vietnam though, as corruption and bureaucracy have not disappeared totally as yet.

The culture of vested interests still stifle the country's potential as shown by the fact that the country's poverty rate has not fallen as rapidly as it should have. Nevertheless, the progress it has made remains impressively striking. The country has become the largest exporter of pepper and is aiming to achieve the same in rice exports. Even India buys tea from Vietnam. With apt policies and more freedom coupled with a transparent democratic government, Vietnam can scale great heights.

From wigs to wealth

In the 1950s, South Korea was as poor as many countries in Africa and Asia. In 1996, it became a member of OECD (Organisation for Economic Co-operation and Development). In other words, it is now part of the rich countries' club. Its GDP per capita is 14 times more than North Korea—its unruly neighbour that has shut itself off from the rest of the world, still enthralled in communist delirium, and fervently believes in the philosophy of central planning, collectivism and self-dependency.

---

8. *The Economist*, The Good Pupil, Vietnam's Economy, Asia, May 06, 2004, http://www.economist.com

9. Asian Development Outlook 2006, *Part 2 Economic trends and prospects in developing Asia*, Vietnam, p. 63, http://www.adb.org

Both countries, South and North Korea, were actually part of one whole but were bifurcated by the catastrophe of the Second World War. They are one people sharing the same blood, same tradition, same culture, same civilization and same language. While one prospered the other withered. South Korea is a vibrant multi-party democracy promoting dissent and debate while its Northern counterpart remains communist under the dictatorship of Kim Jong Il suppressing freedom of speech and denying basic rights to its people. Whereas the South Koreans are successful and cheerfully bustling with riches, North Koreans remain subdued in poverty.

Japan annexed Korea in 1910 and moulded Korean social outlook. The Japanese were responsible for the construction of railroads, highways, schools, hospitals as well as the establishment of modern systems of administration. But they also forced the Koreans off their lands. The Japanese took the top positions leaving Koreans working at the lower level as the majority of them suffered under Japanese rule. The industrial workers and miners employed by the Japanese-owned companies were often treated little better than slaves. Colonial rule resulted in a situation where much of the production of rice went for Japanese consumption.

In 1961 Seoul, the capital city of South Korea, was a pitiful sight. Its inhabitants, an American visitor wrote, "live in miserable jerry-built shacks, and few of them have been able to find jobs. Beggars, some apparently only two or three years old are commonplace, along with vendors who squat for hours on the sidewalks, offering passers-by cigarettes, chewing gum, combs, cheap jewellery, toys, whistles, abaci, and live dogs. The dogs bark constantly; they sound hungry, too."[10]

Enfeebled and enervated under colonial rule, South Korea emerged to become one of modern history's success stories. It rose up from a level much lower than that of Ghana and Congo, and Thailand and the Philippines, it soon went higher up than that of Greece or Portugal by reaching a level comparable with Spain. The government showed shrewd leadership—it understood its limitations and let the market forces shape the country's destiny. The success was mainly due to the private enterprises which took advantage of a favourable economic climate created by the government. From one of the poorest countries of the world some five decades ago, today South Korea shines as the 10th largest economy in the comity of nations. It was once a poor country with an annual income per head in

---

10. Jeffry A. Frieden, *Global Capitalism—Its Fall and Rise in the Twentieth Century,* (New York, Norton, 2006), p. 413

1955 of around $400 (at today's prices), and such poor economic prospects that American officials predicted abject and indefinite dependence on aid. Within a single generation it became a mighty exporter and world-ranking industrial power.[11]

Once an exporter of wigs, it is now the world's biggest shipbuilder; producer of electronics, steel and semiconductors; the manufacturer of globally renowned cars (such as Daewoo and Hyundai) and a world leader in broadband internet. With impressive economic strengths the country did not hesitate to cash in on globalization. The nation boasts a highly skilled and technologically adroit labour-pool.

Like other East Asian countries such as the Philippines and Indonesia, South Korea too had its workers toil in sweatshops making shoes for companies such as Nike. The export earnings went into developing the country's infrastructure and improving education. As productivity and labour wages increased the country focused on producing and exporting higher value-added products thus fully exploiting the benefits of global economy. (South) Korea's government pursued heavy industrial development by sponsoring modern steel mills, chemical factories, and a new auto industry. By the early 1980s the country had the world's largest private shipyard and largest machinery factory.[12]

Ransacked by the Japanese between 1910 and 1945 and locked in a bloody war between 1950 and 1953 with North Korea, it has truly been a blazing march towards prosperity for a country of peasants who were once booted out as dogs by Korea's erstwhile colonial masters, the Japanese. When South Korea hosted the 1988 Olympics, the world got to see the progress that the country had made. A new democratic system was being consolidated, and a popularly elected president shared power with a legislature controlled by the opposition. Beyond the political changes and the gleaming athletic facilities, the country's overall economic advancement was on display.[13]

A number of reasons are attributed to the success of South Korea—sheer hard work; the strategy to export its goods to foreign markets; saving money; making right investments in infrastructure, technology and more importantly, education; encouraging foreign capital, expertise, and investment in the country. Whatever

---

11. The Economist, *Economics—Making Sense of the Modern Economy*, Edited by Simon Cox, (London, Profile Books Ltd, 2006), pp 18–19
12. Jeffry A. Frieden, p. 422
13. ibid, p. 414

the reasons for its prosperity, the fact remains that without capitalism and open markets, South Koreans, who knows, would perhaps still be selling wigs.

The dance of the Elephant

A recent yet promising story is of a country with a billion people, India. It endeavoured, largely unsuccessfully, for over four decades to create national champions. It nurtured the mantra of 'self-dependency' and 'self-sufficiency' but achieved neither. It had several brilliant individuals but was crippled by collective mediocrity. It had a huge market to spur and sustain economic growth but its enterprise remained tied up in bureaucratic red-tape. It relied one-dimensionally on agriculture to fetch economic prosperity, to the detriment of other industries. The country kept falling apart. It practiced a cheap form of socialism that mistook 'liquidation of wealth' for 'removal of poverty' by pouring money into failing government institutions and projects. The end result was not creation of wealth but widespread distribution of misery. It produced sub-standard goods; it let its men, women and children languish in grinding poverty while its centrally-planned economy largely designed the collective fate of the entire population. There was too much planning but very little production. All started to change when the country's leadership—realizing its fast dwindling foreign currency and impending economic cataclysm—opened its economy to the outside world. Privatization and liberalization replaced excessive socialism and government protection.

India had long suffered from the rigid echelons of caste with the 'untouchables' piled up at the bottom of its social strata. India had leaders of men and men of ability long exposed to the outside world, particularly the West, unlike China or Japan before they opened themselves to the world. Yet the country lagged in sloth, lack of enterprise and industry. India had bounteous natural resources. Indian leaders paid lip service to removal of caste barriers while they kept taking roots in the subsoil of Indian psyche. The economic output per capita was miserly in the face of nationalization of Indian economy. For over four decades, the country had encased itself in the ideals of socialism. Its aversion to capitalism, liberalism and privatization stemmed from its allergy to the opening of its economy to the outside world after the long, hard, bitter lesson it learned from allowing the East India Company, or in other words, the British Empire, into its territory which would go on to lay a foundation for the eventual construct of British colonization.

Despite the country possessing several individuals with good technical skills and competency, India as a whole stagnated in its socialist tracks in order to spread wealth across its populace. There was hardly anything wrong with the socialist ideal of communitarian welfare but what wronged the country was the rigid socialist environment in which it was caught up leading to its stunted development. While expatriate Indians in America, Britain, elsewhere in Europe and Singapore, and even in Africa, flourished and became successful as well as becoming significant contributors to their host countries' economies, native Indians in their own country cocooned themselves under the sheath of protectionism, bureaucracy and corruption.

It needed a crisis of sorts for India to wake up from its long economic slumber. The Indian elephant finally stood up after 44 years of vegetation when the country's balance of payments crisis in the 1990s screeched for swift economic reforms. India's inflation, at the time, was running at 17 percent; its foreign exchange reserves humbled as low as $1 billion; its fiscal deficit was staring at about 9 percent of the country's GDP. All began to transform the country as a whole since 1991 when the country's leadership liberalized its economy and has witnessed a sea change in its economic growth as well as in the living standards of many of its teeming millions. According to India's Ministry of Finance,[14] the inflation was brought under control at around 5 percent and the fiscal deficit for 2005 was just above 4 percent. The country's foreign exchange and gold reserves, in 2006, stood at "$165 billion."[15] Official Indian estimates report that poverty fell from 51 percent in 1977–78 to 26 percent in 1999–2000.[16] That is a massive reduction of poverty from half to just over a quarter of total population in a span of two decades albeit at a slow pace considering innumerable opportunities the country had squandered in its dalliance with a centrally-powered economy.

Until the Indian government liberalized its economic policies no foreign investor was keen to take a bet on Indian markets. With a burgeoning middle-class population, a bulging consumer market and booming corporations in Bangalore and Mumbai and other cities as well, the fervour to invest money in India has never been more intense. A growing population, young workforce, free country—the prospects look brighter. Foreign institutional investors poured $30 billion into the Indian market in three years—double the amount they had invested in the previous decade.[17] In 2000 India had a grand total of just three

---

14. The Ministry of Finance, India. For more information on India's Economic Survey and related information, visit its website http://finmin.nic.in/
15. CIA World Factbook, *India*, http://www.cia.gov/cia
16. Jagdish Bhagwati, *In Defense of Globalization*, (New York, Oxford University Press, 2004), p. 65
17. *Time*, How to ride the elephant, (July 3, 2006) p. 31

million mobile-phone users, the precise number that neighbouring China was adding to its subscriber base every month. By the end of 2005, India itself was adding four million users each month, and had exceeded a total of 100 million. Retail explosions like this do not happen very often.[18]

During its flirtatious period with socialism, the Indian government endeavoured to produce 'national champions' who were meant to guide and steer the country onto development. But the 'national champions' only championed their own interests with utter disregard to ordinary Indians. Big companies fleeced consumers, selling shoddy goods for inflated prices. Rather than investing their profits in better technology, they chose to lobby for more special favours from government. Bureaucrats who thought they knew best tied the economy up in red tape—quotas, tariffs, permits, licenses—that distorted incentives, stifled entrepreneurship and bred corruption.[19] With a favourable economic ambience which came through open markets, the government did not have to create 'national champions'. The 'national champions' emerged on their own. Corporations such as Infosys and Wipro grew to worldwide recognition and presence without the governmental crutches.

India's GDP topped $800 billion in 2005. The economy has grown an average of 8 percent over the past three years, the second fastest rate in the world. Its internet-technology industry, which includes other outsourcing services, generated revenues of $36 billion in 2005, up 28 percent in 2004. A surging stock market has boosted the number of Indian billionaires to 23—10 of whom were new (in 2006)—compared with eight in China. Since 1996, the number of Indian passengers on airlines has risen six-fold, to about 50 million travellers a year, and sales of motorcycles and cars have doubled.[20] With the world's largest film industry, a booming tourism sector, a massive Indian Diaspora in the US, UK and elsewhere, the Indian elephant has surely started its dance in the global arena. What India has managed to achieve so far is only a tip of its vast potential. The start has now been made. Thanks to its liberal economic measures, India has set its 'liberalization' spirit free.

---

18. Edward Luce, *In Spite of the Gods: The Strange Rise of Modern India*, (London, Little, Brown, 2006), p. 37
19. Philippe Legrain, *Open World*, (London, Abacus, 2002), p. 68
20. *Time*, 10 ways India is changing the world, (July 3, 2006), p. 25

The Dragon's take-off

Sharing about 7 percent of the earth's land and having around 21 percent of world's total population China has experienced many a roller-coaster ride to be where it is today. As one of the world's oldest civilizations (spanning 5,000 years) that emerged along the Yellow River, China once was a technological leader when Europe was still in the 'dark ages'. The Chinese invented paper; printing; gunpowder. They were also credited with using apparatus for astronomical observation, compasses and water-powered clocks long before Europeans had even thought about them.

When intellectual xenophobia got the better of Chinese rulers they unreservedly turned inwardly. Foreigners soon became objects of fear and hatred. Unlike the Japanese who learnt the tricks of trade and technology from their contacts with the West, the Chinese tried to keep foreigners away from themselves. Supremely confident of their own achievements and immensely contemptuous of foreigners' knowledge, China thwarted itself from making any endeavour to improve upon its scientific and technological advancements it achieved theretofore. The country blindly rested on its past gains and a belief in self-sustenance. The country's introverted attitude soon threw it into technological oblivion, and in the eyes of the West it soon became a butt of political derision and economic pity.

Chinese superiority did not last long and nor did its political stoicism in the face of an inquisitive, acquisitive and aggressive West. The nineteenth century saw the country surrender its trading posts to European countries. Britain, in 1839, arrived in gunboats and brought down the great resistance of the Chinese. Other Western nations followed suit, and then the Japanese, with their own pretensions to dominion after the Meiji Restoration (1868), moved to secure their place alongside Great Britain, France, Germany and Russia.[21] From a height of cultural, scientific and technological superiority, China humiliatingly came crumbling down. Once rich, it progressively became poor. Once mighty, it slowly fell prostrate. Once confident, it disconcertingly stood embarrassed.

Resolved to compete with the west, China finally sought refuge in communism under Mao Tse Tung (also known as Mao Zedong)—but with disastrous consequences! Soon hope was to turn into despair and eventually into widespread misery. The leadership tightened its authoritarian noose. The communist ascen-

---

21.David Landes, *The Wealth and Poverty of Nations*, (London, Abacus, 1999), p. 344

dancy placed emphasis on central-planning—bringing every lever of the country's administration under its totalitarian purview.

In the summer of 1958, Mao embarked upon The Great Leap Forward movement to modernize China's economy through collectivism and mass labour. The project went catastrophically wrong. Mao was convinced that with the vast rural population China would surpass Great Britain's steel production levels in less time and eventually catch up with the West. Some 500 million peasants were organized into large rural communes. Tens of millions were put to work manually building dams and reservoirs, often without the guidance of engineers, who were condemned as bourgeois experts. Mao wanted "the whole people making steel," though he understood little about what went into the process. Within weeks, primitive brick furnaces rose up in agricultural communes, at factories, at hospitals, and in the playgrounds of many of the nation's schools. Peasants, factory workers, doctors, and schoolchildren tried to help meet the party's steel production targets.[22] All done in the name of self-sufficiency! The Great Leap Forward moved inexorably from farce to tragedy. Agricultural yields collapsed, (since peasants were forced to produce steel instead of growing food) and in the early 1960s famine spread across the country. Between 30 million and 40 million people died of starvation.[23] Even as the cataclysm struck the masses, a peremptory communist regime ensured that the "… government faced no pressure from newspapers, which were controlled, and none from opposition parties, which were absent."[24]

Miserably failing in its ambition to outdo the West, China also fell behind its neighbours as South Korea, Taiwan, Singapore and Hong Kong opened their economies by adopting an export-oriented strategy. Death paves way for new life. In China's case, the death of Mao in 1976 brought a new lease of life for China and the Chinese. Mao's successor Deng Xiaoping was sure that the only way to wealth is to open the economic gates of China to the world. And so the great wall of Chinese resistance to open markets was broken down. Wealth creation became the country's first and foremost objective. As Xiaoping himself had remarked, "it doesn't matter whether the cat is white or black, so long as it catches mice."[25]

22.Barbara Freese, *Coal—A Human History*, (London, Arrow, 2005), p. 218

23.John Kay, *The Truth About Markets*, (London, Penguin, 2004), p. 88

24.Amartya Sen, *Development as Freedom*, (Oxford/New York, Oxford University Press, 1999), p. 181.

25.Peter Jay, *Road to Riches or The Wealth of Man*, (London, Phoenix, 2001), p. 14

In 1978, China became an open economy. The farmers had access to the markets to sell their produce. They bought consumer goods. Property rights were established for the first time since 1949. The peasants were returned their household property including farming tools and domestic animals. Local businesses in towns and villages were encouraged as elements of market economy were implemented. Foreign trade and investment were welcomed cordially. Access to technology became possible. Over 20 percent of the population—270 million people—was lifted above the subsistence line in 1978–2000.[26]

China, of course, has not yet attainted its fullest potential. The country still has political and economic barriers to surmount. The countryside lags behind in education, healthcare and infrastructure. Given that 200 million rural Chinese have little or no work they pour into the cities in search of jobs, straining these already heavily populated areas of the country. Certain professions suffer serious labour shortages due to lack of skills. The banking industry is notorious for dishing out bad loans. Pollution is rife. Political freedom still remains a distant dream. The path to full political and economic reform is long and winding.

Beyond its geographical size, China today stands as a mighty country with growing economic clout and political presence. Not for nothing that China is today the third largest automobile market in the world. The country's chip industry may still be in its infancy and pales in comparison with the US, Taiwan, Japan, and Europe but growing electronics and communications and technology industries point to its large growth in the future. China's chip-design industry has grown nearly fivefold, to 450 companies, during the past five years.[27] As a leading producer of colour TVs, mobile phones, desktop PCs, and DVD players, it stands as a consumer-electronics giant. And with 350 million mobile phone users—the most in the world, China today is really talking to the world of its presence.

There are several other star performers on the global economic firmament such as Taiwan, Singapore, Malaysia, Thailand, Indonesia, and Japan who have found their way towards prosperity through international trade, market economy, and global integration. China and India in particular have benefited through integrating themselves with global economy. Neither country was once a champion of free-market capitalism but, whatever progress these two giant nations have made so far has primarily been through global capitalism. The twenty first century seems to belong to them, barring any catastrophe.

Overall, world integration has created more winners and fewer losers.

---

26. Bill Emmott, p. 67
27. *Business Week*, China Ramps Up, (August 22 2005), p. 89

The harbinger of freedom

Freedom and democracy and alleviation of poverty brought about by global capitalism are neither a cruel hoax nor hogwash. The last six decades have been witness to a number of countries engaging themselves with freedom and democracy. Economic freedom plays a pivotal role in both emancipating an individual from material constraints and acting as a means toward achieving political freedom. Capitalism functions on the basic premise of economic liberty. In a capitalist society, unlike a communist society, no individual or group has the authority to initiate physical force against others. As such, the role of the government transforms from being a 'crusher' of individual rights to becoming a 'protector' of those same rights.

Besides paving the way for political freedom, the most creative aspect of capitalism is its ability to let individuals free themselves from the clutches of poverty. A study by Surjit Bhalla, an Indian economist, for the Institute for International Economics called "Imagine There's No Country", confirmed the drop in world poverty. "Measured by the benchmark favoured by the World Bank of income of $2 a day or less, adjusted to cater for difference in purchasing power, the poverty dropped from 56% in 1980 to 23% in 2000.... Thanks to population growth, the absolute number of people in that category remains large: more than 1.1 billion. But that is still far fewer than in 1990 (1.7 billion) and 1980 (1.9 billion). Before 1980, the absolute numbers were rising. That date roughly coincides with the spread of trade and internal-market liberalization to many poor countries."[28] One of the main reasons out of many for the spread of democracy is the spread of institutions of market-capitalism. "Market-capitalism not only resulted in higher economic growth and well-being but also fundamentally altered a country's society by creating a large and influential middle class sympathetic to democratic ideas and institutions."[29]

Economic freedom does encourage a nation's prosperity. This proposition is supported by a study by the Fraser Institute based in Canada in its "Economic Freedom of the World"[30] report. Highlighting the essential cornerstones of freedom such as personal choice, voluntary exchange, freedom to compete and security of privately owned property the study uses 38 components and

---

28. *The Economist*, Liberty's great advance, 28th June, 2003), p. 5
29. Robert Dahl, *On Democracy*, (New Haven/London, Yale NB, 2000), p. 164
30. Erik Gartzke, James D. Gwartney, Robert A. Lawson, Fraser Institute,
    Economic Freedom of the World: 2005 Annual Report

sub-components to measure the degree of economic freedom in five areas: size of the government, legal structure and protection of property rights, access to sound money, international exchange, and regulation.

Researching 127 countries over a period of 30 years or more, the study establishes the strong relationship between economic freedom and prosperity. The freest economies do not just have an average per capita income of $25,062 vis-à-vis the least free ones but also have faster growth than the less free economies. With free countries registering per capita growth at 2.5 percent in the past 10 years, the least free countries could only manage 0.6 percent. Countries with more economic freedom tend to have freedom extended to other areas as well including political.

As economic freedom grows wider, political control becomes narrower—for the betterment of the citizenry. This is quite true of several dictatorships of the past that have today become democracies. Apart from gaining foreign capital, intellectual property, expertise, and technology through economic freedom countries such as Indonesia, Mexico, Chile, South Korea, and Taiwan, for the first time in generations, became democracies. It created a milestone in their respective polities to realize what it would be like to bask in political freedom with nothing much to worry about dangers to their person or their property.

Milton Friedman, the late Nobel laureate, put it succinctly: "Historical evidence speaks with a single voice on the relation between political freedom and a free market. I know of no example in time or place of a society that has been marked by a large measure of political freedom, and that has not also used something comparable to a free market to organize the bulk of economic activity."[31] China, for instance, even though it restricts political liberty, has bestowed economic freedom on its people. Its market reforms and limited increase in economic liberty have changed China's fortunes for the better. China is far from being a free society but it is crystal clear that its residents are far freer and more prosperous than they were under Mao Tse Tung, under whose reign millions of people died for both economic and political reasons. The introduction of liberal economy has undoubtedly created a breathing space, albeit limited yet significantly wider, for many a Chinese at the dawn of the 21st century.

What were once 'command-and-control' regimes are, today, democracies throbbing with vibrant economic growth. Since 1980, according to the United Nations Human Development Report (UNHDR), 81 countries have taken "sig-

---

31.Milton Friedman, *Capitalism and Freedom*, (Chicago, Chicago, 2002), Fortieth Anniversary Edition, p. 9

nificant" steps towards democracy, with 33 military regimes replaced by civilian governments.[32] While some of the countries may have not fulfilled the basic requirements of democracy the point of the matter is that they have taken at least a step in the right direction. Freedom House, an independent non-governmental organisation, in its report on the Freedom in the World, has classified countries, on the basis of their allowance of political and civil liberties to their citizens, as Free, Partly Free and Not Free.

In 1975, according to the data compiled by Freedom House, only 25 percent of countries, or in other words, just 40 countries, were "free". By 2005, it was 46 percent or 89 percent "free" countries. During the same years, the total number of "partly free" countries had risen from 53 to 58 in total. But the percentage of "partly free" countries had fallen from 34 percent in 1975 to 30 percent in 2005. The "not free" ones too had fallen in 1975 from a total of 65 (41 percent) countries to 45 (24 percent) in 2005.[33] It is important to note that the drop in the percentage of "partly free" countries even when the total number of "partly free" countries was higher is due to the emergence of several new countries. Since 1990, thirty new countries have been created as a result of the dissolution of the USSR and Yugoslavia.[34]

There is no country in the annals of history that has ever achieved social prosperity through economic unfreedom. Burma is an unenviable specimen for its military notoriety in ruling its citizenry through intimidation and violence. The egregious human rights abuses, gross violation of justice and individual freedom, coupled with the military's allergic attitude to foreigners and free trade strangulate any significant economic exercise to cater to the basic needs of its 'exploited' populace presents composite evidence of how lack of freedom can destroy a country.

Ordinary Burmese do not even have economic freedom, let alone political freedom. The ruling military junta is overwhelmed by fear that granting economic freedom to the country's *hoi polloi* may ultimately lead to the erosion of its political power. Burma's "... pervasive corruption, nonexistent rule of law, arbitrary policymaking, and tight restrictions on imports and exports all make Burma

---

32. *The Economist*, Liberty's great advance, p. 5
33. Freedom House, *Freedom In The World 2006*, Selected Data from Freedom House's Annual Global Survey of Political Rights and Civil Liberties.
34. About.com, *New Countries of the World, The 30 New Countries Created Since 1990*, Jan 2, 2006, http://geography.about.com/cs/countries/a/newcountries.htm

an unattractive investment destination and have severely restrained economic growth."[35] Where economic unfreedom stands in the way of people, freedom from poverty too stands unattained.

Does economic liberty promote political freedom? China, still an authoritarian country, cannot avert granting its citizens elements of freedom thus making them less dependent on the state. Canopied with tension between balancing economic and political freedom, China may, sooner or later, have to give in to one way or the other: either to allow more political freedom to its people as two decades of economic growth have provided hundreds of millions of Chinese a greater say in the running of their lives, or revert to curtailing their economic growth through stringent political measures. It is a choice between a freer country ensuring wider prosperity or a more controlling regime exposing itself to the vagaries of change, resistance and uncertainty.

Economic freedom is a powerful force in encouraging political freedom. The fact that political freedom has not happened in places like economically-free but politically-authoritarian Singapore is an exception rather than the norm. The economic success of China or Singapore or pre-democratic South Korea, for instance, did occur not because they curbed political interests to their citizens. Their economic success was primarily due to "helpful policies" such as "… openness to competition, the use of international markets, a high level of literacy and school education, successful land reforms and public provision of incentives for investment, exporting and industrialization. There is nothing whatsoever to indicate that any of these policies is inconsistent with greater democracy."[36]

Economic freedom provides a favourable environment to infuse wider freedoms extending to polity but without a strong rule of law neither economic freedom nor political liberty will bear fruit. With unclear rules of law or absence of laws many poor countries remain illiberal both on economic and political fronts. Countries like Zimbabwe and Pakistan are not averse to open markets. Yet benefits of market liberalization have greatly bypassed a majority of their people. Or, their leaders crassly abuse power through acts of omission and commission. In both countries 'cosmetic' democracy has taken over 'functional' democracy. Both countries 'conduct' elections but suppress political freedom.

---

35. Heritage, *Burma (Myanmar), Index of Economic Freedom 2006*, http://www.heritage.org

36. Amartya Sen, p.150

Even with opportunities created by open markets and globalization, govern-ments and leaders of poor countries such as Zimbabwe and Pakistan stand in the way of letting the markets work to their advantage. In Zimbabwe, starting with its leader, Robert Mugabe, the whole administrative machinery is filled with par-asitic leaders swarming in the misery of their poor citizens, and whose locust appetite for plunder and malversations of their office have left their country rav-aged, flogged and ravished. Pakistan, for its part, has all its powers concentrated in the hands of General Pervez Musharraf who, under his supervision, conducts elections but decides the contestants in those elections. The cases of Zimbabwe and Pakistan are common, in varying degrees and patterns, among several pov-erty-stricken places in Asia, Africa, Middle East and parts of Latin America. It is the 'pillage of the public' engineered under the 'tag' of democracy.

Several nations today, in different measures, are trying to achieve both eco-nomic freedom and liberty. Former erstwhile blocs of the Soviet Union such as Estonia and Lithuania have achieved economic freedom and are now strengthen-ing their young democratic foundations. Whether a country is a rich and mature democracy or a developing and strong democracy or an economically dynamic authoritarian society, the central role of economic freedom in fashioning a freer society is obviously manifest.

Not fracturing, but bridging

In the early 1990s, (Albanian) women were raped over and over by Serbian guards; also, the men were forced to castrate their fellow prisoners. In all thou-sands were tortured and executed. In Rwanda in 1994, ordinary Hutus killed eight hundred thousand Tutsis over a period of three months. In Jakarta in 1998, screaming Indonesian mobs torched, smashed, and looted hundreds of Chinese shops and homes, leaving over two thousand dead. In Israel, the same year, a (Palestinian) suicide bomber driving a car packed with explosives rammed into a school bus filled with thirty-four Jewish children between the ages of six and eight. On September 11, 2001, Middle Eastern terrorists hijacked four American airplanes. They destroyed the World Trade Center and the southwest side of the Pentagon.[37] A dreadful concatenation of global events! Apart from their violence there is a connection between these episodes. The answer lies in the relation-ship—increasingly the explosive collision—between the three most powerful forces operating in the world today: markets, democracy and ethnic hatred.[38] So

---

37. Amy Chua, *World On Fire*, (London, Arrow, 2004), p. 5
38. ibid, p. 6

writes Amy Chua. There is also another scaremongering: "At present global markets work to fracture societies and weaken states."[39] So too writes John Gray.

The spectre of collision of markets, democracy and ethnic hatred on the one hand, the fracture of societies and weakening of states by global capitalism on the other hand, is more than adequate for mob-led anarchists to set the 'world on fire' and to convince them that the promise of globalism is a 'false dawn'. It is amazing how random events, regardless of where they happen, when they happen or how they happen, are all attributed to a single cause—global capitalism—with utter disregard to history when people, for thousands of years to this day, have still been fighting, killing and bombing one another in the name of religion; in the name of ethnicity; in the name of politics and the list could go on *ad infinitum*. War and strife among humanity is not a recent phenomenon and is not whetted singularly by the rise of global capitalism.

The Durants (Will and Ariel Durant) wrote in the year 1968 that "in the last 3,421 years of recorded history only 268 have seen no war."[40] Going by the arguments and logic of Chua and Gray that global capitalism is the cause of societal violence and fracture, global capitalism must have been in existence for nearly three and a half thousand years causing, spurring or propelling every war. The world has, by no means, since 1968, been free of violence, war and collision either. The world, post-1968, has seen several terrors and turbulences right from the then ongoing US-Vietnam war that broke out in 1965; the suppression of uprising in Czechoslovakia, called the Prague Spring in 1968; the Indo-Pakistan war again in 1971 that led to the liberation of today's Bangladesh, and its birth, from the exploitative fangs of Pakistan; the extension of Vietnam war well into the mid-1970s; the execution of millions of Cambodians by Pol Pot from mid-1970s to 1979; the Iran-Iraq war in the 1980s; invasion of Lebanon by Israel again in the 80s; the continuation of South African Apartheid until early 1990s; the Gulf war between the US and Iraq in the early 90s; the bombing of World Trade Center in 1993; US military actions in Somalia in 1993; and the Rwandan genocide to the suicide attack on America in September 2001, and to the ensuing invasion of Afghanistan and Iraq later at the break of the 21st century as an ongoing mission of "War on Terror". The *raison d'être* for gleaning a few instances of global tumults and trepidations from the recent past and paint them as phenom-

---

39. John Gray, *False Dawn—The Delusion Of Global Capitalism*, (London, Granta, 2002), p. 196

40. Will and Ariel Durant, *The Lessons of History*, (New York, Simon & Schuster, 1968), p. 81

ena of global capitalism with an anti-globalization brush is at best—puerile and at worst—malevolent. The world has been never been free of collision, nor societies without fracture. And, it would be a summit of paranoid illusion to hope that abandonment of global capitalism would usher in permanent peace and serenity on earth.

What does it mean to the world of the stability of a region comprising of about 40 percent of world population? What would happen should a war break-out in a region always seeming to be on the boil in a cauldron of political unrest, religious acrimony and ethnic diversity? What would happen if one or two or all of the three nations in the region blanketing a sea of humanity and, in possession of nuclear weapons, should declare a nuclear war on the other? The countries in question are the flashpoints of the world today—for reasons both good and bad—they are China, India and Pakistan. One is a communist country with largely homogeneous culture. Another is a democratic country with a mosaic of diverse cultures and ethnicities and languages. The third is a highly volatile Islamic nation identified along its two main sects—Sunni and Shia.

On one side, the political relationship between China and India has hardly been convenient. Below that calm exterior, that is being exuded of late, by both Chinese and Indian leaders, an undercurrent of mutual suspicion always keeps streaming steadily. The bitter uneasiness between the two giant nations of Asia started over territorial disputes leading to a war in 1962, souring relations between the two countries for decades. When things seemed to be getting normal towards the approach of the millennium, the then defence minister of India, George Fernandes jejunely described China as India's arch enemy. In an interview to the BBC he said: "there can be no let-up in our defence priorities as far as China is concerned."[41] The comment jolted both the Chinese leadership as well as India's when it was normalizing the relations between the two countries.

Against the odds of provocative rhetoric and mutual suspicion, the two countries have travelled a long way today as not to let petty politics submerge their hard-earned economic development under the weight of mutual antipathy. Both countries have become cautious of each other's sensitivity. The imbecility of the past has given way to a new-found maturity of the present. It is said that India's leadership in 'software' and China's eminence in 'hardware' are tuning together melodiously to create a symphony. Though slightly exaggerated, that may be hard to dispute. The annual bilateral trade between the two countries soared

---

41.BBC, BBC News Online, *Fernandes fixates on Chinese threat to India*,
    Thursday May 7, 1998, http://news.bbc.co.uk

"... from a paltry \$190m in 1990"[42] "... by 80 percent to reach \$13.6 billion[43] (in 2004). There is increasing awareness—especially in India—that, far from competing in a zero sum game, both countries are growing at such a speed that there is enough room for each to accommodate greater productive capacity. "People used to say it was China and not India, then it was China against India—but if you look at any number of sectors the real story is more likely to be China and India," says N. Srinivasan, head of the Confederation of Indian Industry.[44]

Mutual distrust may still be lingering between the friendly vibes sent across by both countries but the realization that peace is constitutive of long-lasting economic well-being is gathering momentum. As Cheng Ruisheng, a former Chinese ambassador to New Delhi, says: "We both need a peaceful environment to develop our economies."[45] That underlines the weighty sway that international trade holds both nations in a peace-mould which had long remained zealously estranged as one stayed passionately communist and the other, flirtatiously socialist.

On the other side, two countries, India and Pakistan, emerged independent and disfigured in 1947 after Robert Clive established the British Empire through the supremacy of the East India Company in 1757, from the yoke of British colonial rule through ghastly bloodshed, wholesale killings, and heaps of human misery piled up on either side of the border. It set off a panic infested with migration of innocent peoples across the two countries. The flow of refugees became a flood; word of atrocities, rapes and mass killings brought the inevitable retaliations. As the violence escalated, ghost trains chuffed silently across the new frontier carrying nothing but corpses. In the 'land of the five rivers' the waters ran with blood and the roads ran with mangled migrants.[46] It was not prompted by American-fed global capitalism nor fashioned by modern day globalization. The animosity between Hindus and Muslims dates back to the time of Babur's invasion of India in the 16th century, the founder emperor of Mughal-Empire in India. Aurangzeb, a latter Mughal Emperor epitomized the 'austerity' of Islam which saw 'intolerance' of anything and everything, that was non- or un-Islamic,

---

42. *The Economist*, Clash of the titans, (November 4, 2004), http://www.economist.com

43. *The Economist*, Too early to tell, (April 14, 2005), http://www.economist.com

44. *Financial Times* (US), Edward Luce and Richard McGregor, China and India benefit from trade growth, 23 February, 2005

45. ibid

46. John Keay, *India: A History*, (London, Harper Collins, 2001), p. 508

at its apex. His misrule pinnacled with harsh punishments of non-Muslims yoked with their secondary status in the society; destruction of non-Muslim sites of worship; and sweeping conversions of non-Muslims into Islam. His epoch inseminated the sharp Hindu-Muslim polarization, only to turn out to be a fodder for the exploitative British East India Company to further divide Hindus and Muslims and later to establish the British Empire. Traces of that ill-will between modern India and Pakistan do extend right to this moment with a dash of ugly politicking. Aurangzeb's rule was pure plunder and insensitive intolerance that was common among tribal groups during the Middle Ages in different parts of world with a strong pinch of madness for religious propaganda and conversion. No research has yet been done to see if any 'hint' of "global capitalism" pitted Muslims against Hindus or vice versa during Aurangzeb's rule.

For a large part of their existence as independent countries, the relation between India and Pakistan is marred by rhetoric of animosity, haggling over ownership of Kashmir, India's charges of Pakistan of fomenting terrorism and an interspersion of military conflicts. The present day Indo-Pakistan conflict is largely an inheritance of their unsavoury history, much less to present global economy. If there is any thaw that is currently carving the relationship between the two countries, the credit must largely go to the popular consensus in both countries that cross-border commercial trade is crucial to ameliorate their relationship.

When India's parliament came under a 'suicide attack', India summarily posted its soldiers along the Indo-Pak border. The sabre-rattling of unleashing nuclear weapons assumed the centre-stage. Soon, a million troops from either side of the geographical divide were staring eyeball to eyeball. Eventually, common sense prevailed in both countries considering the impact a war would have on their peoples, their livelihoods and their economies. Up to now, both countries have taken a series of confidence-building measures to put their problems in perspective and resolve them. A growing sense of economic interests among Indian and Pakistani businessmen urging their respective governments to promote trade as well as people-to-people contact became a vital force that factored in the eventual weathering of a searing political climate.

Hiccups have always been part and parcel of Indo-Pakistan relationship from accusation to counter-accusation on issues from terrorism to access to nuclear material to normal every day political bickering. The underlining fact is that the 'economic' interests of both countries, the danger of reverting to economic ruination, and the possibility of loss of bulging 'foreign direct investment' in both countries, tempered the volatile situation wisely. The dangerous situation brought not only the leadership of China—the immediate neighbour which feared the possibility of its economy suffering as a consequence should a war breakout between India and Pakistan—but many of the world's leading players including the U.S. and Britain rushed to urge calm and peace between the two countries. Such was the impact of the relevance of international trade. It was a triumph, a significant one at that, of how global economic interests can muster immense political judiciousness to establish peace when deployed prudently.

There are numerous other prickly political relations between countries which are kept to a minimum mainly due, not by any wisdom-driven diplomacy, but to economic interests fuelled by international trade and sensitivity. China has long been threatening Taiwan of dire consequences for the former sees the latter as a renegade island that should be part of mainland China. Despite thorny exchanges tinged with Chinese military threats, trade between the two countries has kept expanding and growing. Indirect trade between Taiwan and China rose 23.8 percent year-on-year to 46.32 billion US dollars in 2003.[47] A war, (between China and Taiwan) would come at a terrible economic price, not only for Taiwan but for China too. And one thing Chinese officials seem to agree on is that the party's (communist) grip on power (in mainland China) depends on a vibrant economy.[48] The economic fortunes of both countries were earned not through self-sufficiency model of economic growth but through international trade; through integrating themselves with the world economy; and through their constant pursuit of global wealth. The global capitalism that catapulted both countries to the status where they are now is also holding them back from any military conflict, excepting China's customary political-browbeat tactics.

The twilight of the Second World War left Europe wearied, wrecked and exhausted. Before the stroke of the war and at the height of its power, Nazi Germany had controlled its neighbouring states under the conviction that it could achieve economic efficiency through the creation of special economic zones. Poland, for instance, became Germany's backyard for exploitation and plunder. The first half of the twentieth century saw several European states warring against one another. Indeed, between 1870 and 1945, France and Germany fought three wars.... Britain took part in two of the wars; Belgium and the Netherlands were invaded in the same two; Italy fought on one side in the 1914–18 war and

---

47. Yahoo News, Australia & NZ, *Taiwan-China trade up 23.8 percent in 2003 despite political standoff,* Tuesday 2nd March, 2004
48. *The Economist,* Survey: Taiwan, The dragon next door, January 13, 2005, www.economist.com

another in that of 1939–45.... Europe's twentieth century is thus justifiably and conventionally seen as a story of the perils of nationalism and of its ugly sister, racism.[49]

The catastrophe that plagued Europe after the First and the Second World Wars heralded an urgent need and determination to rebuild Europe from the ashes of destruction. The desire for peace and stability was overwhelming. There was also an earnest determination to avert the possibility of another war by bringing several European countries under one umbrella. And, precisely for that reason the European Coal and Steel Community was founded in 1951 to pool the steel and coal resources of the member states together. It later evolved from a mere trade body into an economic and political partnership which is today's European Union bristling with a membership of 27 countries with 490 million citizens. Justifiably, a cardinal purpose of the European Union is the prevention of war. The great wealth of the existing EU was built (during) 1950–90 on the liberalization and integration of just half the continent, one that was divided by the ideological and military barrier of the Iron Curtain."[50] Ever since the Iron Curtain disappeared, the potential for wider trade, plus new and closer relationships, looks greater with the integration of more countries from the erstwhile Soviet bloc. The driving force behind the birth of EU was to achieve economic integration thereby avoiding political disintegration.

The history of the European project since its launch after World War II was one of fitful advance toward greater depth and breadth of integration through the process of institutional adaptation and the inevitably messy business of political bargaining and compromise.[51] It brought the continent its peace, wealth and progress. Any conflict, today, is hardly imaginable between European nations waging war against one another apart from the democratically-driven, regular political arguments, and parliamentary debates to express national issues of member states. It is economy, first and foremost, that is keeping Europe bound together. That, precisely, is one of the focal reasons why Turkey, a Muslim country, is attracted to and charmed into, and yearning to be, a part of a booming Europe.

---

49. Bill Emmott, p. 106

50. ibid, pp103–4

51. Michael Mendelbaum, *The Ideas That Conquered The World*, (New York, Public Affairs, 2003), p. 372

Doing the business

Legal rigidities have a tendency to feed extension of poverty. Over-protectionism, over-cautiousness and over-possessiveness do not necessarily flower out of care and concern. Such tendencies also sprout out of unfounded fear and misguided insecurity. The best of intentions may also bring out the worst of results. Socrates' intention to make the youth think rationally led him to the consumption of hemlock, and, eventually, to his death. The litany of economic regulations of 'welfare-minded' developing as well as poor countries, even though it may be meant to protect workers and to control individual enterprise, often handicap the unskilled and the poor who otherwise would benefit from 'any' job instead of having 'no' job. Economic despotism of a government prevents individuals imbued with the spirit of entrepreneurialism from kick-starting the developmental process through business and employment generation. Unnecessary, burdensome and excessive regulatory environment are only capable of furnishing individuals with a passport to further poverty.

"Doing Business in 2005", a report by the World Bank, highlights the obvious dampener of how heavy regulations asphyxiate wealth creation—wealth creation through creating job opportunities, encouraging businesses to move into the formal economy and promoting economic growth. The study highlighted three main findings: 1) Businesses in poor countries face much larger regulatory burdens than those in rich countries. They face three times the administrative costs, and nearly twice as many bureaucratic procedures and delays associated with them. And they have fewer than half the protections of property rights of rich countries. 2) Heavy regulation and weak property rights exclude the poor from doing business. In poor countries 40 percent of the economy is informal. Women, young and low-skilled workers are hurt the most. 3) The payoffs from reform appear large.[52] The more a country's business environment is bandaged with red tape the likelier it is to be poor. In such an environment the exercise of setting up a business—without experiencing the rigmarole of legal hurdles, paucity of credit facilities and unwritten laws of running a business and a widespread malaise of corruption—becomes more an exercise of self-flagellation than an encouragement of self-support for an enterprising individual.

It would be naïve to believe that there are saintly men running the government with welfare of people illuminated in their bosom. It would be too optimis-

---

52. World Bank, *Doing Business 2005: Poor Nations Struggle To Reduce Red Tape For Business, Miss Large Growth Opportunities*, http://www.worldbank.org

tic to hope that honest leaders can make policies work even if they are entangled in a web of regulations. Officials generally have a tendency to usurp public money. Kautilya, the author of Arthashastra, in ancient India, remarked way back in 400 BC that "just as it is impossible not to taste honey or poison when it is at the tip of the tongue, so it is impossible for a government servant not to taste a bit of revenue". It holds true even in the 21st century particularly wherever the net of regulation is spread far and wide. In poor countries, regulations are often in the wrong place—difficulty in securing a loan; no property rights; fat bureaucracy; cumbersome laws; prolonged process; rampant corruption and an unwritten law to bribe officials and much more. Sadly, there is hardly any regulation to ensure bureaucratic transparency; official accountability; and, simple business processes. Burdensome regulations often encourage graft. The more frustrating the rule, the more likely is the attitude to bribe officials to move files.

Just how time-consuming and difficult it is for a migrant to start a small business on the outskirts of Lima (Capital of Peru), Hernando De Soto[53] highlights the legal obstacles ingrained in the procedures. It took 289 days to start a perfectly legal business. The cost of legal registration was $1,231—that is 31 times the monthly minimum wage. Obtaining legal authorization to build a house on state-owned land took six years and eleven months—requiring 207 administrative steps in 52 government offices. To secure a legal title for that piece of land comprised 728 steps. In other countries, such as Philippines, Egypt and Haiti the bureaucratic obstacles, the number of years it takes to register a piece of land and the amount of legal hurdles to overcome are no less formidable than in Peru. It takes 153 days to start a business in Maputo, but 2 days in Toronto. It costs $2,042 or 126 percent of the debt value to enforce a contract in Jakarta, but $1,300 or 5.4 percent of the debt value to do so in Seoul. It takes 21 procedures to register commercial property in Abuja, but 3 procedures in Helsinki. If a debtor becomes insolvent and enters bankruptcy, creditors would get 13 cents on the dollar in Mumbai, but more than 90 cents in Tokyo. Borrowers and lenders are entitled to 10 main types of legal rights in Singapore, but only 2 in Yemen.[54]

Weak property rights, restrictions and the ambition to doing business remain light years away in numerous developing countries. Property rights are almost taken for granted in countries where the legal structure is developed and judiciary efficient. Almost anyone living in rich or working democracy can use a property

---

53. See Hernando De Soto's 'The Mystery of Capital—why capitalism triumphs in the west and fails everywhere else', (London, Black Swan, 2001), pp. 18–23.

54. The World Bank, Doing The Business in 2005, See Above

as collateral to raise a loan. A formal property structure also helps people know their rights and the availability of opportunities that exist in a uniform system. It provides an opportunity for would-be entrepreneurs to transact with strangers, share knowledge with others when information on property, registration process, transaction costs and legalities become freely available. Such facilities are common in the West, which are conspicuous by their absence in poor countries. High transaction costs discourage people from risking whatever assets they own. The solution is to simplify business entry, slash barriers to entry and provide titles to property.

The myth that social protection requires more business regulation deserves an outright rebuttal. Countries choosing to have fewer regulations do not have to stamp out social support. The Scandinavian countries have an enormous human development and economic prosperity in spite of managing an enviable welfare state. The businesses in Scandinavian countries are among the least regulated. Canada, though welfare-oriented with state-funded healthcare for all, encourages any willing entrepreneur to register a business quickly. These countries focus their regulations where they should matter—protecting property rights and providing social services. Estonia, Latvia and Lithuania, having gleaned the best principles from their richer neighbours, are among the countries with benign business environment. Loyal pursuit of benighted regulatory ideology would not elevate masses reeling in poverty. What is needed is common sense assessment and informed debate as to how to make things work. Market reforms do not have to be carried out at the expense of destroying the social safety net. Both can work together.

Protectionist itch

The benefits markets elicit depend not only on what they can do but also on what they are allowed to do. There are businesses that profit immensely without the need to tamper with the markets. There are businesses that profit only through protection of their markets lest their established interests should be undermined. The latter often use their political clout to ensure that markets are restricted to sustain their narrow interests even though they reap minuscule benefits. Protectionism is a five-pronged trade barrier that comes in the form of 1) providing *Subsidies* to protect businesses from succumbing to risks related to costs, 2) raising *Tariffs* to restrict foreign goods—which also includes anti-dumping tactics, 3) reserving *Quotas* to prevent the flow of foreign goods which otherwise would find favour with consumers, 4) offering *Tax Cuts* to reduce costs of domestic businesses and 5) *Intervention* of state to rescue failing businesses despite inefficiency.

Whichever barrier a government chooses the burden invariably falls on the consumer who has to pay more for goods and services.

It is not uncommon among interest-groups to indulge in 'China-bashing' with the singular aim of keeping intact their protectionist interests. Should any economic woe betide the West or America, China becomes the favoured whipping-boy as a monstrous guzzler of oil and stealer of manufacturing jobs. Japan shared similar honours when its trade surplus with America spiralled in the 1980s. Soon it could be India, as many service-oriented jobs have started finding an easy route there. It is indeed an irony that rich countries extol the virtues of free-market mantra when it comes to selling their produce abroad but sing paean when it comes to protecting their own 'markets', 'workers' and 'farmers'.

Protective pampering

A new affectation pervades the American psyche to blame emerging countries for the slow-demise of their manufacturing sector. Deeper diagnosis reveals that it is not a slow-demise as such but a decline of a sector long exposed to productivity, high labour costs and a shift in consumer spending habits. The impact caused by international trade on American manufacturing industry is minor compared with the general ills that afflict the sector at large.

Even before the growing clout of globalization, the number of workers employed in manufacturing kept falling steadily in a downward fashion. In 1950, value added in the manufacturing sector accounted for 29.6 percent of gross domestic product (GDP) and 34.2 percent of employment; in 1970 the shares were 25.0 and 27.3 respectively; by 1990 manufacturing had fallen to 18.4 percent of GDP and 17.4 percent of employment.[55] A shift in consumer spending from 'manufactured goods' to 'services' has further acerbated the pain. In 1970 US residents spent 46 percent of their outlays on goods (manufactured, grown, or mined) and 54 percent on services and construction. By 1991 the shares were 40.7 and 59.3 percent respectively, as people began buying comparatively more healthcare, travel, entertainment, legal services, fast food and so on."[56]

Higher productivity means 'cheaper goods' and 'unemployment'. Increase in productivity occurs not as a result of trade, but of advance in technology. When an industry becomes more productive, it produces more goods with fewer workers as 'automatons', for example, do a significant amount of jobs more efficiently

---

55. Paul Krugman, *Pop Internationalism*, (Massachusetts, The MIT Press, 1996),
    p. 36
56. ibid, pp. 39–40

than people do, and more quickly. A worker with a computer today can do a pay-roll job in a matter of hours that a clerk, thirty years ago, would have taken days to do the same job. A robot can weld more automobile chassis in an assembly line far more efficiently and quickly than a couple of workers doing the same job taking longer hours. A crane has the ability to hoist and move, in little time, a heavy piece of timber, which would otherwise require the brute strength of twenty men and more time. In spite of machines taking up jobs and being responsible for job lay-offs there is hardly any murmur demanding a total ban of computers or robots or cranes. Technology, the principal usurper of untold number of jobs, is rarely cursed for loss of jobs yet the complaint goes misdirected, bafflingly and wrongly, at global trade.

Amidst the uneasy angst about the decline of manufactures and the blame placed on China for 'manufacturing ills' which are largely home-grown, rich countries' obsession with agricultural subsidies is particularly telling. Farming, doubtless, is one of the earliest and oldest economic activities but now is in the thrall of ever-decreasing output and employment. Europe spends about €50 billion ($58 billion) a year to protect its farmers, through a Common Agricultural Policy (CAP) which results in higher prices of farm and agricultural products for its consumers. The agricultural subsidies consume about half the European Union budget for a farming work force comprising less than 5 percent its total workforce.

The CAP, in short, is a double-edged public-policy misadventure hurting both consumers in rich countries and the farmers in poor countries. The CAP, in effect, raises labour costs by preventing cheap imports of food from abroad. The consumers end up paying higher costs for products which could be imported cheaply thus helping the poor farmers in developing countries. The taxpayers shell out their money only to cradle less productive farmers through subsidies in the arms of their pampering governments. Subsidies keep food prices in rich countries far above world prices. It hurts farmers in poor countries whose cheap farm and agricultural produce, as a result of farm subsidy and irrational protec-tion of 'inefficient' sectors in rich countries, are effectively prevented from being sold in international markets and are harmed further by the dumping of subsi-dized rich-country products into their own countries.

Notwithstanding such governmental extravagance of rich countries, the income levels of farmers have drooped inexorably. France's agricultural share is 2.7 percent of GDP and has a workforce of just 2 percent. Britain's share is 1 per-cent and 1 percent respectively. In Germany, 3 percent of farmers contribute towards 1.1 percent of GDP. Japan's 5 percent of farmers contribute 1.3 percent of GDP. It makes little sense to lavish money on a withering breed of farmers who in the US produce just 1.4 percent of GDP with a workforce of 2 percent. Euro area as a whole has 2 percent of farmers working in agriculture with a contribution of 2 percent of GDP.[57]

The stance taken by rich countries' to protect their markets is both 'autocratic' and 'hypocritical'. Autocratic, because the European Union, North America, and Japan wrote and rewrote the rules of the international economic game as they wished, with no input from the four-fifths of humanity living elsewhere. It is hypocritical because despite high-sounding rhetoric about open economies and free trade, the north imposed continuing obstacles to southern exports. Most egregiously, Americans, Europeans and Japanese stepped up colossally expensive programs to protect and subsidize their own farmers, then preached the wonders of the marketplace to developing countries.[58]

Patently blocked

Just as people own physical objects or properties, they are also entitled to own the ideas they conceived. When such ideas transform into books, movies, or music they benefit the public in general. But conflict of interest arises when the inventor or conceiver of a product or service endeavours to earn profit out of his invention and when the public wants to acquire the inventor's product or service free, or at the lowest price possible. Any inventor seeks some incentive to further invention. Curb that incentive, and the urge to continue to more invention drains away. This is where patent assumes greater significance.

Patents offer temporary monopoly rights and ownership over new products, processes and techniques to their inventors by the government. Patent protection is an important tool employed to foster further technological progress in order to enable inventors as well as innovators to recoup research and development investment and costs, then secure a reward in the form of profits for their invention. To prevent monopolistic exploitation, patents are allowed to remain for a limited period only so that the invention eventually becomes universally available to everybody without having to pay further incentives to the inventor.

James Watt's steam engine, Einstein's theory of relativity and Vivaldi's four seasons were not invented with profit in mind. Nor did the inventors keep their inventions to themselves. They let them operate freely in the public domain for everybody's benefit. The world, today, works on an entirely different plane.

---

57. *The Economist*, Pocket World in Figures, Country Profiles, pp107–245
58. Jeffry A. Frieden, p. 469

While costs of research and development have grown huge, competition has become fierce. This is particularly so in the area of drugs and medicines.

In spite of spectacular discovery and invention of medicines and drugs, mankind has not completely achieved a permanent subjugation of diseases. There is no guarantee whatsoever that humanity will ever prevail over the evolutionary nature of bacteria and viruses which seem to be giving birth to new strains of diseases. Organisms that survive complete extinction evolve resistance to the drugs we use against them. We shall need to go on finding more and more sophisticated drugs against the bacteria and viruses of the natural world, in an evolutionary guerrilla war that we can hope to contain but never to win.[59] It is in this context that incentives for drug firms become vitally crucial.

A steady flow of invention of goods and services is essential for social progress, human welfare and better living standards. In such a scenario, poor countries are not equipped nor do they have the financial resources and expertise to invent or purchase expensive products. More than 3.5 million people in Africa succumb to diseases, such as TB and malaria that are humanly preventable. Ten thousand Africans die needlessly and tragically *every single day* ... of AIDS, TB and Malaria.[60]

What prevents the prevention of preventable diseases to the poor, especially those ailing in poor countries? Affordability. While patent is important for allowing companies to recoup their research and development costs and to earn profits to channel them for further invention, patents, especially in the realm of pharmaceuticals, have become a tool for exploitation and means to plunder fat profits at the expense of millions of world's poor. Many poor Africans, for instance, do not have the means or money to buy the drugs needed to combat treatable diseases such as TB and malaria. About 3 million Africans die due to AIDS-related illnesses. In many parts of Africa, AIDS cocktails are unaffordable even at low prices. Only a very few countries qualify to get drugs at low prices and there are only a very few of them who can afford to buy those drugs.

When major pharmaceutical companies noticed that their rivals in the developing world were copying their drugs and selling them at cut-throat prices, they threw their weight into preventing the supply of cheap drugs to poor countries. Charging the pharmaceutical firms in the developing world with epithets such as 'thieves' and 'pirates', drug firms in the West wormed their way into the WTO

59.Paul Seabright, *The Company of Strangers*, (New Jersey, Princeton, 2005), p. 116
60.Jeffrey Sachs, *The End of Poverty*, (London, Penguin, 2005), p. 215

(World Trading Organisation) to play patent-politics. The WTO, whose main purpose is to encourage international free trade by untangling regulatory cob-webs, started playing to the notes of Western drug corporations by threatening their poorer rivals in developing countries with sanctions. TRIPS (Trade-related aspects of intellectual property rights) became a stick in the hands of big western drug companies to discipline their rivals in the developing world. For virtually the first time, the corporate lobbies in pharmaceuticals and software had distorted and deformed an important multilateral institution, turning it away from its trade mission and rationale and transforming it into a royal collection agency.[61] If free-trade is all about competition and consumer welfare through low-prices, TRIPS is manipulated to exactly do just the opposite. It replaces competition with 'monopoly' and consumer welfare with 'consumer exploitation'.

The issues are more complicated than they, at first, seem. Several issues and interests surround patenting rights. Without patent, a drug firm may become less inclined to invest into research and development of new drugs to fight ever evolv-ing diseases and infections. Supplying drugs gratis will be beyond common sense as drug firms invest billions of dollars to invent a new drug after it goes through several stages of trial and error. Yet, the profits that drug companies make dwarfs the costs sunk in the production of drugs. Nevertheless, four concerns besiege the question of patent:

First, allowing drug firms in poor countries to replicate those invented by rich countries could slash potential profits of rich-country drug firms. Second, low profits or loss of potential profits could discourage or even hamper investments into further research and development to invent new drugs especially for diseases harming third-world countries. Third, drugs sold at a very cheap price in poor countries may tempt patients in rich countries to buy drugs cheap in poor coun-tries, which may further whittle down profits and incentive to invest. Fourth, by normal standards, the poor in Africa cannot afford drugs even at local prices.

Patent protection, though, has its own reason for its existence in the eyes of high-income countries for the reasons mentioned above it largely remains a rent-collecting device. It is particularly so in the case of drugs and medicines which poor countries have a dire need of and a necessity of access to. It hardly reflects common sense, let alone compunction for the poor who not only have to shell out thousands of dollars a year on drugs to combat curable diseases such as Malaria and TB, when the patent period is applied uniformly across all countries when they are so different in their income levels and earning capacity.

61.Jagdish Bhagwati, p. 183

The patent protection, as it stands today, is anything but balanced. There are two sides to the politics of patent protection. One is about reaping returns on invention as well as recouping costs of research and development. The other is about spreading the benefits resulting from successful invention of, say, drugs and medicines. If the rich drug firms are focused on the former, it is the poor countries that would yearn to see the reality of the latter. Therefore, finding a balance between the two is of paramount importance.

When patent-politics takes the centre-stage of WTO it weakens its case for free-trade which it fervently claims to espouse. The WTO is all about freeing trade. The TRIPS agreement is about restricting it. Tearing down trade barriers exposes companies to greater competition—and so means lower prices for consumers everywhere, not least poor countries. Enforcing global intellectual-property standards reduces competition in poor countries—and so raises prices for those who can least afford to pay. For that reason, not only should the TRIPS agreement not be at the WTO, it should not exist at all.[62] The rules muscled in by the drug firms inside the portals of WTO are clearly and needlessly aimed at harming poor countries.

Diseases hurting the poor in the developing countries are indeed formidable. Combating diseases requires multitudinous efforts. True, the problems are daunting but are solvable with proven technologies and practical strategies. A combination of international cooperation—from making availability of drugs to the poor, to financial aid to working towards a realistic time frame is needed to tackle, through the following seven measures, the outgrowth of disease in the poor world.

First, where possible, poor country governments could share some of their costs by eradicating embezzlement of public funds, which is rampant in developing countries of Africa, Asia and Latin America.

Second, rich countries could do away with their farm subsidies and divert some of the funds towards the purchase of drugs in poverty-stricken, disease-prevalent countries. Such a move would not only help the disease-stricken populace in poor countries, it would also benefit consumers in low-growth Western countries through cheaper imports of goods.

Third, TRIPS must be tripped out of the WTO. It defies the very reason for which the organisation exists. Competition among drug companies can be increased by freeing up trade, not by excessive patent protection but a realistic

---

62. Philippe Legrain, p. 266

patent protection that takes into consideration the economic realities of different countries and their desperate need for goods and services.

Fourth, countries such as Brazil and India with manufacturing capabilities of generic drugs should be allowed to produce drugs to sell in poor countries.

Fifth, big drug firms with tighter controls in poor countries could actually sell drugs at a cheaper price instead of imposing a blanket refusal to sell drugs in poor countries. Earning a marginal profit by selling drugs to the poor is nonetheless better than not selling, thus losing profits and inciting local drug firms copy their drugs.

Sixth, rich countries must increase their annual aid to poor countries so as to enable them to buy drugs and help them meet basic necessities of life.

Seventh, and foremost, the fruits of capitalism must reach the poor unhindered. While it is true that people are sick because they have no job to earn money and cure their illnesses, it is also true that they cannot work because they remain sick and infirm due to their poverty.

CHAPTER 2

▼

THE APPEAL OF
DEMOCRACY

The subjugation of Germany and Japan in the Second World War and the collapse of the Soviet Union four decades later curtailed the spread of dictatorial rule and the domination of communism thus saving the world from a possible alienation of human rights and freedom. The enfeeblement of communism and the erosion of dictatorship supplemented the rise of democracy as an ever increasing number of people had come to realize the value of their freedoms and rights in the realm of polity. Over the years, many countries have metamorphosed into democracies by granting economic, political and social freedom to their citizenry. Even those countries that hesitated, or were outright reluctant, to identify themselves with democracy, more or less, have adopted the tenets of democracy. Erstwhile eastern European communist regimes, for instance Ukraine, Estonia and Lithuania, have moved towards democracy; even Russia, for long a hegemon of Slavic states, has unshackled itself from the confines of communism; China keeps whittling down its communist roots to adjust itself to the changing global scenario.

Human society embeds a sharp polarization of interests created by individuals' conflicting goals, values and visions. Commonality of interests is an unattainable luxury even in a homogeneous society, let alone a heterogeneous one. Imperfect that we are, we constantly pull and push ourselves in different directions in order to fulfil our needs and wants. Divergence of interests invariably constructs a ground ripe for discord among both individuals as well as groups. Therefore, the likelihood of encroaching upon the rights and interests of a fellow citizen always remains thick and strong. Conflict and cooperation are twin facades of any society. The concentration of one or the other very much decides the course of an outcome. There will be either progress or stagnation. An increase in conflict will quite stall any room for further progress. Conversely, a willingness to cooperate tends to encourage progress.

Weaker members of a society are often vulnerable, possibly because they form a minority group. In Malaysia, ethnic Chinese and Indians are unequal vis-à-vis their native Malay brethren, whilst in Sudan the Arab north is economically better off than the Christian and the animist south. Historically, they may be deprived of basic opportunities, as in apartheid South Africa or caste-driven India where the low-caste Indians were, and are still in certain parts of the country, alienated from social gatherings and prevented from entering the temples, so protection of their rights becomes paramount. No man attains his fullest development so long his rights are denied and his freedom curtailed. No system other than democracy can guarantee such a right. Democracy defines the rights of both the rulers and the ruled provided the 'rule of law' prevails in the society.

Therefore, the challenge of moulding the interests of different individuals or groups of individuals through mutual consent, compromise, and cooperation is to find a common ground with the rest of the population. This must be done in such a way that the interests of the majority are fulfilled to a large extent without harming the status of minorities while offering the minorities the right to protest within accepted norms of equality and degree of freedom. Where there is no democratic right it would result in a society where the formidable easily tramples upon the rights of the less formidable.

Democracy functions through the vote of the majority but its fairness ensures that the minority rights do not fall by the wayside nor do they become crushed even though the majority decision counts greater. Democracy offers means for the minority to raise its concerns through democratic institutions if it feels that its rights are affected and interests are diluted. A strong democracy constitutes elements such as fair and regular election, right to free expression, right to form associations, and a free media. Besides, a truly active democracy is regarded to have effective opposition political parties, accountability of government, rule of law, independent judiciary and guarantee of rights to individual and property.

More 'perfect' than the rest

The cardinal purpose of democracy is to guarantee human rights and fundamental freedoms and ensure that executive and legislative powers are executed in accordance with the wishes of the electorate through their elected representatives. Fulfilment of such purpose of democracy is itself meritorious in its own right. Over the course of history, democracy stood up as a bulwark against totalitarian establishment such as monarchy, dictatorship, and communism. The reason why more than half the world embraced democracy is that democracy is considered more suitable than other types of government. Like any system of government that is far from 'perfection', democracy is no exception either. Where democracy is different to the rest of governance is that it is the more viable option available to common people.

The defects of democracy are less ruinous than other forms of government. The human costs spilling out of authoritarianism easily surmounts even the miseries caused by war or disease or famine. Paranoid fears of 'conspiracies' against his dictatorial regime forced Joseph Stalin to unreservedly decree people to imprisonment. Adolf Hitler was directly responsible for the disappearance of six million Jews including their genocide. Benito Mussolini force-fed his dissidents into guzzling castor oil. Idi Amin engineered the ethnic cleansing, largely Asians from Uganda, for he was 'ordained' to do so by an 'angel' in his dream. Pol Pot massacred more than two million people for a largely stupid reason that he simply feared Buddhist monks, individuals wearing glasses, and Western-educated intellectuals. In the absence of democracy, it is only too easy for the *hoi polloi* to fall prey to individuals captivated by bizarre fantasies and psychotic fears.

Democracy is sometimes disparaged as a mere 'formal' freedom bestowed upon citizens during the time of an election. In truth, it is this 'formal' freedom which actually confers on people the right to judge and to dismiss a failing or failed government without coup or bloodshed. It is this 'formal' freedom that is conspicuously missing in other forms of government. It is this 'formal' freedom that provides people with the power to protect themselves from abuse or misuse by their governments. Despite years of struggle to be free and despite the granting of economic freedom to create wealth, ordinary Chinese are still tied in political chains. To express a fair criticism of a government policy, an ordinary Chinese is bound to weigh his words so as not to find himself in a cell mulling over his fate. The irony is that the communist leaders do not even tolerate the use of certain words as they are unlawful to use in the country. When Google, the search engine, set up its Chinese website it censored its search services to satisfy the mandarins in the communist hierarchy. Google censors its services so that Chinese people cannot search for terms such as 'democracy, Falun Gong' and other topics the administration considers offensive and against its policy.

When thousands of Chinese students and workers protested at Tiananmen Square in 1989 against Communist government's corruption and political repression, it only resulted in the brutal deaths of many protestors at the hands of armed soldiers. The estimates in civilian deaths, from official to unofficial, vary from 400 to 7000! Dissidents of democracy vociferously pinpoint the 'weaknesses' of democracy often with a revolutionary verve while remaining deaf-mute to the atrocities committed upon peoples in autocratic regimes. Not beyond a murmur is heard from the opponents of democracy on the pompous tyranny of North Korean government over its people as they remain locked in poverty and their freedom stridently manacled. This is where democratic institutions let the 'formal freedom' play its unique part. The periodic 'formal freedom' bestowed upon people allows them to overthrow callous and careless and corrupt governments without fear. Where such formal freedom is absent it confers an unchecked license for the government officials to do what they want with arrant impunity and in utter disregard to their citizens' wishes.

When the Bharatiya Janata Party (BJP) government in India ignored the plight of several impoverished farmers, it was duly voted out for it failed to see the misery of impoverished farmers at the grassroots level. The ousting of the party came as an utterly unexpected shock in the face of its overall economic achievements when India was registering a GDP growth of about 7 percent and over 10 percent in the IT sector alone, thus earning oodles of political goodwill on the global political arena. The government became enamoured of its own outer achievement and the dazzling growth of the IT sector but stood blindfolded to the deeper travails of the poor who kept plummeting into ever deepening debts that led to dozens of suicides of enormously indebted farmers and their families.

Despite the higher contribution of the IT industry to Indian economic growth it (IT sector) employed just 800,000 people when 35 million of the workforce is unemployed.[1] The electoral drubbing that the BJP received was more conspicuous in the two states, Andhra Pradesh and Karnataka, known for their superstar status in the IT boom and for the glittering info-tech hubs and call centres in their capital cities, Hyderabad and Bangalore respectively. The electoral defeat of the BJP conveyed a valuable lesson that elections in democratic societies come

---

1. *Sunday Observer*, Economic growth must benefit the poor, Features, 11th July 2004, http://www.sundayobserver.lk

not too often but when they do come they provide a powerful weapon to the voiceless to voice their frustration.

No country, by right, becomes 'democratic' because it prefers to call itself so for the reason that democracy is appealing and popular. Robert Mugabe, the leader of Zimbabwe, calls his country 'democratic' and thinks he is running the country 'democratically'. He runs elections. Zimbabwe has a parliament. But, the truth is that Zimbabwean democracy exists only on paper. In practice, Mugabe tames his opponents. He drives white farmers out of their lands in the name of 'land reform'. He lives a lavish life, and so do his cronies, while the poor in his country starve. Amy Chua in her book "World On Fire" complains about "... 0.6% of (the) white population owning 70% of the land"[2] in Zimbabwe. While it may be true that white population owned a majority of land nothing had prevented the majority black Zimbabweans from owning the land and competing with the whites. The minorities (whites) run the economy and they are the engine of Zimbabwe's economic growth employing over two million people in their farmlands. Where the government failed to create jobs, the white farmers created them instead. To blame only the minority whites for all the social ills created or neglected by the government highlights a blinkered vision to the problem. If minority whites had usurped land illegally or if they had committed any crime, law must have taken its own course duly. A working democratic country does not 'create' laws to victimize a section of its own people and cloaks its own failures and inefficiencies by accusing a section of people for 'exploiting' the prevailing conditions better than the rest.

A sensible approach calls for bettering the lives and improving the skills of the rest of the population. Progress depends on 'levelling up' and certainly not on 'levelling down'. Ordinary Zimbabweans have low literacy rate; they lack basic health care; many are unemployed. To blame the white farmers for government inefficiency, administrative sloth, widespread plunder, and bureaucratic corruption is a futile exercise to scapegoat the minority farmers. White minority farmers did not stand in the way of universal education. They did not block universal health care. They did not rant against creation of jobs by the government. There are few fundamentals which the government ought to do. Democracy does not stand in the way of fulfilling the basic needs of a society. When the leadership is rotten, it does not make any difference whether the system is democratic or otherwise. At least, in a democracy, people have a hope and an opportunity to topple 'looting' governments and 'perfidious' leaders. Democracy works when people let it work.

---

2. Amy Chua, *World On Fire*, (London, Arrow, 2004), p. 102

It is a slap in the face of those living in democracies and those who have voluntarily embraced a democratic way of living to hear that they are brainwashed into consenting since "… it is necessary to control not only what people do, but also what they think."[3] It is akin to saying that adults are incapable of thinking on their own. It is tantamount to denigrating human intelligence. The lower-caste people had long been oppressed under social divisions by upper-caste Hindus in India for hundreds of years. The exploited outcastes would still have remained in the mires of exploitation but for democracy. It is the instruments of democracy available to them such as media, judiciary, benefit of franchise, and support groups to lend voice to their tribulations that fashioned a significant change not only in their social standing but also their mainstream participation in national politics and economic contribution.

The marginalized sections of the society, of late, have found voice and confidence through the instruments of democracy that they uninhibitedly demand their leaders to provide their villages with roads, electricity and hospitals. Under the caste-infested India of the past, the unprivileged and the untouchables listened to their leaders with heads bowed-down and arms folded. In a resurging democratic India the same unprivileged and untouchable people make their leaders listen to them. According to S L Rao, former Director of the National Council of Applied Economic Research, "People at the lowest levels find their votes make a difference, and they are exercising their difference."[4] The change is occurring because the lower castes are acquiring more literacy, a little more prosperity, and greater access to mass media. Government-run affirmative action programs—called "reservations" in India—have hastened this transformation.[5] Centuries of scavenging, serving, and slaving of the untouchables on the most bottom of the social hierarchy now have significantly been erased by the presence of democratic edifices. In comparison with any feasible alternative to it, democracy has at least ten advantages such as avoiding tyranny, essential rights, general freedom, self determination, moral autonomy, human development, protecting essential personal interests, political equality, peace-seeking and prosperity.[6]

---

3. Noam Chomsky, *Noam Chomsky Reader*, Edited by James Peck, (London, Serpent's Tail, 1988), p. 132
4. *Business Week Online*, The Rise of India's Lower Castes: Turmoil and Promise, 20th May, 1999, http://www.businessweek.com
5. ibid
6. Robert Dahl, *On Democracy*, (Yale NB, 2000), p. 45

Asian Values and Democracy

The so-called "Asian Values" argument championed by 'self-interest' promoting leaders such as the former Prime Minister of Malaysia, Mahathir Mohamad, and the former Prime Minister of Singapore, Lee Kuan Yew is an attempt to justify the rule of an autocratic system with a singular purpose to muffle any sort of opposition or dissent. Mahathir Mohamad's adherence to "Asian Values" was an attempt to cover up his own scant regard for human rights and to sustain his authoritarian rule that lasted for about 22 years without effective opposition. Lee Kuan Yew, the founding father of Singapore, invoked his assertion of "Asian Values" as something common to Asian societies such as placing importance to discipline rather than rights and conformance to authority rather than questioning the leadership.

The idea of "Asian Values" comes from the Confucian thought that the interests of society or nation must be held above those of individuals. But, in truth, the interpretation of Confucianism to defend the argument of "Asian Values" is selective and deviant from its purported meaning. The reading of Confucianism that is now standard among authoritarian champions of Asian Values does less than justice to Confucius's own teachings. Confucius did not recommend blind allegiance to the state. When Zilu (an impetuous disciple of Confucius) asks him 'how to serve a prince,' Confucius replies: 'Tell him the truth even if it offends him'.... Lee's application of Confucianism was not a direct reflection of his personal perspective or his desire to integrate its principles, but instead an extension of his desire to utilize religious ideology as a tool for (political) manipulation.[7]

As Nobel Laureate Amartya Sen emphatically argued, "the nature of Asian values has often been invoked in recent years to provide justification for authoritarian political arrangements in Asia. These justifications of authoritarianism have typically come not from independent historians but from the authorities themselves (such as governmental officers or their spokesmen) or those close to people in power, but their views are obviously consequential in governing the states and also in influencing the relations between different countries.[8]

---

7. Uri Gordon, *Machiavelli's Tiger: Lee Kuan Yew and Singapore's Authoritarian Regime*, Department of Political Science, Tel-Aviv University, March 2000, http://www.singapore-window.org

8. Amartya Sen, *Development as Freedom*, (Oxford/New York, Oxford University Press, 1999), p. 231

The argument of the ilk of Lee Kuan Yew and Mahathir Mohamad is that 'Asian' culture is different from 'Western' culture hence the leaders need not be accountable to their people; that their leaders know what is best for their society; that they are like fathers who know what is good for their children.

Whatever Singapore has achieved has been through crushing political dissidents to dust; through chaining the lives of people to rigid laws and; through treating human rights as non-essential. The apparent bottom line of such 'moralizing' talks is that it is purely self-serving. It is no coincidence that the foremost advocates of undemocratic governments in Asia are the same individuals who run those governments; indeed, because freedom of speech does not exist in their societies, it's hard to know what their people really want.[9] Interestingly enough, Amy Chua proudly highlights the "alluring exemplar" of Singapore's "… astounding rise of prosperity, modernity and civil stability"[10] by hiding the shady discriminatory practices subtly existent and the country's ruling family's hold of economic interests of the country. It is no wonder that the rulers of Singapore diligently champion the 'family values' slogan so that the country's wealth is shared among the family and passed on from one generation to another.

Singapore is now globally renowned for its exclusive brand of legitimized corruption and nepotism. How on earth one could legitimize the 'lawful' suppression of people and holding of country's wealth by a single family? Lee Hsien Loong, the Deputy Prime Minister of Singapore is the elder son of Lee Kuan Yew, the founder of Singapore. Loong is married to Ho Ching, who was appointed to head Temasek, "a government holding company that is the most concrete expression of Singapore Inc. Temasek owns (in effect) controlling stakes in 20 of Singapore's biggest companies and many smaller ones. Ms Ho is spectacularly well connected. Quite apart from her powerful father-in-law and husband, her brother-in-law, Lee Hsien Yang, also happens to run Singapore Telecommunications (SingTel), Temasek's and Singapore's largest company.[11] Apart from nepotistic corruption, there is another discontent brewing under the veneer of 'clean' Singapore—the subtle racism actively promoted by the majority Chinese. Increasingly, though, the government has increased the country's "Chineseness" (through) the intensification of the annual 'Speak Mandarin Campaign', the

9. David Scott Orr, AWorldConnected.org, *Globalization and Democracy*, 15 August, 2003, http://www.aworldconnected.org

10. Amy Chua, p. 262

11. *The Economist*, Whither Singapore Inc?, 28th November, 2002, http://www.economist.com

repeated call for Chinese to have more babies, the big budget for Chinese drama serials on television, the insistence that the Chinese proportion of the population must stay and may reach a maximum of 76%, a liberal immigration policy designed to bring in some 100,000 Hong Kong Chinese to Singapore, the official patronage for Confucian studies and the building of Chinese theme parks and entertainment centres by Hong Kong tycoons."[12] Amy Chua would do well to look into blanketed muzzling and nepotistic ransacking of its people and wealth before waxing extolment on, perhaps, her favourite country, Singapore.

There is no way to clearly know whether people actually yearn for freedom in authoritarian countries, mainly due to the glaring fact that they cannot speak out. Autocratic countries do not hold elections; do not encourage free media; and, hysterically control the thought-processes of their citizens. Hence, it is unsound to state that citizens in authoritarian countries are indifferent to political and democratic rights. No individual dares speak out his mind if political threat looms over his head. To take silence for consent is to destroy an individual in silent oppression. The abasement of fundamental freedoms is truly the cherishing philosophy of leaders in many third world and authoritarian countries but to jus-tify that as to be the 'will' of the people is an extravagance. It must be noted that India in 1975, under Prime Minister Indira Gandhi, orchestrated the infamous 'emergency' to silence the opposition through arrests and censorship, and to introduce reforms such as family planning and clearing the slum dwellers through force. When she called an election to justify her draconian measures, the Indian electorate—among the poorest in the world at the time—duly voted her and her party out of power. To claim that poor people do not generally care about or do not require political and civil rights is to make a mockery of their feelings to be free.

Democracy and economic well-being

The apex of cold war in the twentieth century between America and former Soviet Union did not just limit itself to the confines of military might. It was also a race to economic prosperity. The ensuing experiences and events of post-cold war exposed the stark reality of countries notorious for economic unfreedom and political unfreedom, becoming poorer and by comparison countries which pro-moted wider economic and political freedoms, prospering by leaps and bounds.

---

12. Linda K Fuller, *The Role of Dominant Ethnicity in Racism: Reportage on Chinese Rule in Multi-Racial Singapore*, The Edge, The E-Journal of Intercultural Relations, Summer 1998, Vol.1(3)

The gist of this argument is to stress the point that democracy and economic prosperity lead one to another and societies that are both democratic and economically free have more chances of sustaining long-term human prosperity than those that are economically and politically un-free as well as those that are economically free but politically unfree.

Today the belief in some intellectual circles that material prosperity does not hinge upon political liberty is starting to gain currency especially after the rapid rise of communist China, authoritarian Singapore, oil-rich Arab states, and a resurgent Russia where people are granted economic freedom with a defined and sometimes largely undefined stately control on their political dos and don'ts. The view that a country can be run indefinitely by granting economic freedom on its subjects without guaranteeing political freedom is nothing more than a myopic delusion.

It is argued by the supporters of authoritarian governments such as those of Singapore and China that democratic freedom pointlessly empowers the opposition parties, gives excessively unnecessary rights to individuals and considers a mélange of differing interests that together contribute to the hampering of economic progress. The limited examples of Singapore and post-reform China are two countries mostly cited by the critics of democracy. Such examples cannot be taken very seriously for the reason that they can be contradicted by the examples of India and Botswana. India, with all its differences and social hierarchies, is registering spectacular economic growth as more and more of its businesses are exposed to foreign competition while "Botswana has been an oasis of democracy on that troubled continent"[13] of Africa. Much of how a country functions depends precisely on its circumstances and how people work together. In fact, some of the main reasons for China's better performance have nothing to do with the political system. When China started its reforms, in 1978, it was poorer than India. Part of the gap now is due simply to that earlier start. Well before its pre-reform days China had already "… done a more impressive job than India did in educating and providing health care for its poor. Reforms benefited from what economists call "good human capital", and from a bulge in the working-age population that India itself is now experiencing."[14]

The success of East Asian countries owes more to the policies such as openness to competition, investment in healthcare and literacy of their peoples, viable land

---

13. Amartya Sen, pp. 149–150

14. *The Economist*, The tiger in front, 3rd March 2005, http:// www.economist.com

reforms, and industrialization than to authoritarianism. None of these policies stand in the way of greater democracy. Moreover, a country's GDP alone, achieved through economic growth, is not a true measure of human welfare in that country. It is also important to look the widespread availability of freedom for people and opportunities to exercise their capabilities.

It is worth noting that the Human Development Index commissioned by the United Nations Development Programme (UNDP) which assesses the economic requirements of life expectancy, adult literacy rate, gross employment ratio for primary, secondary and tertiary schools and GDP per capita, shows that the top 24 places out of 177 countries surveyed for human development, are occupied by strong democratic countries committed to both economic and political freedoms, transparency in their political institutions, independent media to freely scrutinize and criticize the policies and programmes of the government if need be, and the upkeep of civil liberties. The report divided the countries surveyed into three groups as those with "high human development", "medium human development" and "low human development".

According to the Human Development Index 2006 rankings, the much hyped-up authoritarian regimes of Singapore and China rank well behind several active democratic countries at 25th and 81st places respectively, proving the benefits that come with strong democratic governance, and economic freedom. Countries with medium, as well as low human development are predominantly those either with flawed democracies practiced in raw forms or those with authoritarian regimes.

Since both economic and political freedoms are vital for the full development of societies it is important to recognize the fact that for long-term prosperity one without the other would be significantly insufficient. If authoritarianism has worked economically well in Singapore and relatively successfully so far in China the same cannot be said of countries where neither economic freedom nor political liberty has worked. Put differently, both market reforms and democratic experiments have failed in countries where the system of rule, perception of free markets and individual freedom are in constant conflict with each other.

Economic freedom in African countries, for example, in Côte d'Ivoire (popularly known as Ivory Coast) is largely synonymous with widespread plunder of national wealth, corruption, bribery, and tribal warfare. Whereas democracy in the Middle East is taken as a license to violently express blind allegiance to one's sect as it is happening in Iraq where imposed democracy has greatly been a failure despite the much publicized election in that country.

Take the case of Côte d'Ivoire. No amount of market reforms and resources seem to lift the country out of its instability. It is the richest country in West

Africa, and has the fourth-largest economy of (anywhere) south of the Sahara.[15] It used to be a stable country in a region lacerated by war. The country was once ruled by Félix Houphouët-Boigny, a relatively benign but corrupt dictator, since the country's independence from the French in 1960. In the first two decades after independence, Côte d'Ivoire's annual growth in real terms was more than 7 percent a year, placing it among the top fifteen countries in the world. The results could be seen in the towering office blocks which dominated the skyline of the capital, Abidjan, in the neat plantations stretching for miles over the countryside, and in the thriving market towns inland. So impressive was Côte d'Ivoire's economic progress that it was termed a 'miracle'.[16] Houphouët-Boigny let immigrants from other African countries, insisting them as brothers, into the country and to work. Though Houphouët-Boigny put the country's economic agenda on top he himself set a bad precedent at the helm disregarding democratic norms.

Houphouët-Boigny appropriated one-tenth of the revenues from the country's cocoa exports and distributed part of misappropriated funds to his cronies. He also exempted members of his family and clan from paying taxes, provided them with high-level state jobs and offered them easy credit terms for business. No matter how honest a leader's intention to make his country economically prosperous, when he tries to usurp a lion's share of the country's wealth it paves a way to ruins. Lack of democracy in Côte d'Ivoire despite Houphouët-Boigny's wish to transform the country's economy only resulted in destruction when the commercial environment changed globally.

One of Houphouët-Boigny's grand schemes was to transform his home village in Yamoussoukro into a new capital city with grand buildings. During the 1960s and 1970s Yamoussoukro received more than one-third of total urban investment outside Abidjan. The presidential palace he built there was sometimes referred to as an African version of Versailles. At the entrance stood two gold-painted rams, Houphouët's personal symbol. Sacred crocodiles were kept in the palace pond, fed daily on live chickens, and a sacred elephant was allowed to wander within the walls. Houphouët also built himself a basilica modelled on St Peter's in Rome, at a cost of $145 million.[17] Soon the extravagance evaporated

---

15. *The Economist*, The melting-pot cracks, 3rd Oct, 2002, http://www.economist.com

16. Martin Meredith, *The State of Africa*, (London, Simon & Schuster, 2006), p. 285

17. ibid, pp. 288,289

into thin air as the international prices for coffee and cocoa plummeted leading to an increase in government debt and falling incomes.

Run as private fiefdoms of the ruling elite, their products required huge government subsidies: prices for sugar were three times the world price, prices for rice were twice the world price. In 1980 more than half of public external debt was attributable to ten parastatal organisations.[18] Should such leadership have ever taken place in a proper democracy it would not have survived the patience of the electorate, or the public in general. The security provided by democracy may not be missed so much when a country is running smoothly as when Houphouët-Boigny did not face any challenge to his leadership; the security offered by democracy may seem less relevant when outside conditions are favourable as when the country's leadership took for granted the high demand for coffee and cocoa as a bounty from nature on which it could depend perennially.

After the death of Houphouët-Boigny, Henri Konan Bedié, a xenophobe, succeeded him, and proclaimed the policy of 'Ivoirité', thus appealing to national and tribal prejudices while granting land ownership to native Ivorians and barring foreigners from voting. In 1999, his government was overthrown in a military coup helmed by General Robert Guei. The following year, Guei held elections, which were blatantly rigged, and excluded prominent opposition leader Alassane Ouattara that made Guei able to declare himself the winner.

Popular protest saw Guei step aside, ultimately bringing Laurent Gbagbo, runner-up in the elections, into power. Ivorian dissidents and disaffected members of the military embarked on a futile coup attempt in 2002. Despite peace initiatives, Côte d'Ivoire, still remains far from permanent peace and is treading along the thin edge of civil tensions. By no means, the conduct of farcical elections and the selection of one dictator after another through electoral rigging and sham elections could ever be endorsed as democratic. At no stage were economic interests allowed to flourish in a country that is among the world's largest producers and exporters of coffee, cocoa beans and palm oil. A situation continually worsened by civil unrest would only fetch dire repercussions. Neighbouring countries depend on remittances from migrant workers in Côte d'Ivoire which eventually could affect the former economically. The dire situation in Côte d'Ivoire is an outcome not of democracy but atrocities inflicted by despotic leaders in the name of democracy which never existed in the first place. No economic growth ever occurs in a society shredded by communal savagery.

---

18. ibid, p. 289

Democracy, in short, is not a hindrance to poverty. Rather, it accelerates a country's progress towards overall human development. Barring very countable exceptions of authoritarian countries, most of the rich countries are committed to democracy and market economy. The poorest country in the 30-member Organisation for Economic Co-operation and Development (OECD) club is Turkey with GDP per capita of $4,810 which is way far ahead of 9 percent growth-registering China's GDP per capita of $1,700 while the richest among them is Luxembourg with a GDP per capita standing at $62,700. Luxembourg is a tiny country which was once, heavily dependent on steel but increasingly diversified its economic reliance to include chemicals, rubber and financial services. Most of Luxembourg's banks are foreign-owned and carry out international transactions. It is a country enjoying the fruits of extraordinarily high standard of living coupled with a distinction of having the world's highest GDP per capita. Democracy is a valuable ideal worth pursuing. In unison with sound economic strategy, basic freedom, justice, and equality, democracy protects people from the tyranny of authoritarianism and totalitarianism thereby creating a path towards both economic prosperity and individual well-being.

Another argument that people do not value political freedom but only economic freedom holds true only, and depends solely, on what they value the most in a given situation. When people are poverty-stricken and facing mass starvation, it is natural for them to opt for 'economic freedom' instead of 'political freedom' as survival becomes an urgent priority as against mere proclamation of political rights. Thrown between two alternatives of survival and freedom, one would certainly prefer the former. It is not a question of what people want to choose. It is a matter of what *reason* they have to choose. Because survival-needs pre-empt freedom, freedom cannot be denied on the basis of a belief that 'government-knows-best' ideology and therefore freedom is irrelevant.

Democracy and Islam

After 9/11 the Bush administration had made it a vow to export democracy to the Muslim word. A virtuous vow though it did not seem harmful at the beginning. In fact, there was hardly anything wrong with the idea of spreading democracy in the Islamic world. The efforts to democratize the Islamic world especially those in the Middle East and Arab region were intended to bring freedom to hundreds of millions of people, especially women, suppressed wrongfully in the name of religion.

As the development of unsavoury events and incidents plunged the Middle East into chaos, in particular Iraq into chaos, democratization of Islamic countries was dismissed as an anomaly to Muslim countries which in fact it was not. In truth, it was not democracy that plunged the region into ever more chaos but the manner in which America went about imposing democracy in the Islamic world that turned out woefully wrong as the tactic (use of force and coercion) that was employed to spread democracy, brought only more resistance and more hatred towards democratization of Muslim countries. The noble idea of bringing freedom and liberty to disadvantaged and suppressed peoples in the Muslim world, unfortunately, came to be seen as part of America's 'war on terror' strategy designed to establish American hegemony in the Middle East.

The 'freedom agenda' initiated by the Bush administration in spreading the values of democracy across the spectrum of the Islamic world came to represent, in the eyes of sceptical Muslim leaders, scholars, and intellectuals alike, a veil for larger American interests in the Muslim world for oil, power, and an imposition of its culture. America toppled the Taliban in Afghanistan and Saddam Hussein in Iraq where its urgent goal was to bring about democracy. Sadly, in both places democracy has taken a severe drubbing. Democracy has not succeeded in either country yet as factional and sectarian killings are still rife. In the case of Iraq, the main reason for invasion was to unearth the Weapons of Mass Destruction (WMD) that Saddam Hussein was accused of hoarding but when the investigation found no WMD, the Bush administration, and Blair government too, conveniently moved from the talk of WMD to making ordinary Iraqis free from the iron clutches of Saddam Hussein. The 'freedom agenda' in Iraq has been hit by a serious setback as Sunni radicals are so adamant in not letting up their intermittent but regular bombing of Shias and Shi'ite places of interest while Iranian Ayatollahs are busy sharpening their political tools to have wider control on Iraq. Even the bungled trial and the botched execution of Saddam Hussein do not appear to let democracy flower in a country poised to disintegrate further.

The current political climate raging across the Middle East and in several other Muslim countries is deeply ridden with scepticism of wider American political ambitions that even its good intentions are widely interpreted as pretensions. When America talks of human rights, of persuading Islamic regimes to allow political dissent, and of granting more media freedom in Muslim countries it just provokes radical Islamists to invariably and spontaneously rise up to threaten local governments against caving in to American pressure. The control of radical Islam in some Muslim countries is so totalitarian that is fundamentally difficult to change or reform unless the radical establishments themselves become sensitive to the plight of their peoples. Every attempt by America to bring democracy to the Muslim world is seen through the goggles of suspicion that it only seems to fetch more bad than good. Instead of weakening the influence of regimes such as Iran and Syria, America's debacle in democratizing Afghanistan and Iraq, eventually emboldened them while gifting Iran a strategic advantage in the region as it could keep the unrest going to its east in Afghanistan and in the west in Iraq, while making America bleed with little or no cost to itself.

The present times are testimony to the fact that the more America tries to bring democracy to the troubled Middle East the more anarchy, militancy and terrorism it seems to bring along with its efforts. The general Middle Eastern perception over America's efforts to democratize the entire region is that the latter has a hidden agenda to economically, politically, and militarily dominate the region by using the idea of 'democratization' as a ploy. The disenchantment resonates beyond the political corridors. Despite America's efforts to democratize Iraq, the toppling of Saddam Hussein's regime and the holding of elections which brought to power the majority Shias after years of oppression under Saddam Hussein, a great majority of Iraqis have hardly warmed to America's "favour". An opinion poll conducted in Iraq in 2006 suggested that 90 percent of Iraqis would refuse to live next door to Americans, pinpointing the aversion of America beyond politics.

When President Bush talked about the "crusade" against terrorism, in no time it rang alarm bells in Europe and the Muslim world. It revived the fears of a clash of civilization. Despite the dousing of the flames by Bush clarifying that the "true face of terror is not the true faith of Islam" and "that's not what Islam is all about", the word "crusade" had already given an impetus to the winds of hatred and distrust. The statement was potent enough for the fundamentalists to exploit it to their advantage. They saw it as an attempt by the Christian world to mount unjust military operations on the Muslim world. The talk of "crusade" further set the spread of democracy back in the Muslim world. Where the Bush administration made a serious error was not in its goal of spreading democratic values, universal freedom, and liberty but, as mentioned earlier, the manner in which it went about implementing it and the obnoxious fallout of 'war on terror'—prisoner abuse in Guantanamo Bay and Abu Ghraib.

Often, another argument goes: democracy does not suit Islamic countries hence they should be exempt from democratization and left alone. The Saudi monarchy's most articulate spokesman, Prince Bandar bin Sultan, often reminds American officials that if they press his government too hard, the likely alternative to the regime is not Jeffersonian democracy but a Taliban-style theocracy.[19]

---

19. Fareed Zakaria, *The Future of Freedom*, (New York, Norton, 2003), p. 120

It is further argued that "the Arab rulers of the Middle East are autocratic, corrupt, and heavy-handed. But they are still more liberal, tolerant, and pluralistic than what would likely replace them. Elections in many Arab countries would produce politicians who espouse views that are closer to Osama bin Laden's than those of Jordan's liberal monarch, King Abdullah.[20] To say that individual freedom and liberty do not matter to people in Islamic countries is not just flawed but also short-sighted because the existing rulers are better than the likes of Osama bin Laden.

Democratic elections may well one day bring someone like Osama bin Laden to power or vote an al-Qaeda government to power and wage a war on America or the rest of the non-Islamic world. So far, there is no evidence to prove that this has happened. Having attempted an insurrection in Saudi Arabia, al-Qaeda is growing less popular there.[21] The suicide attack by an al-Qaeda suicide bomber in Saudi Arabia in 2004 made bin Laden an outcast in his own country. In Palestine, the militant Hamas, despite its call for expunging Israel from the region, has not carried out any large-scale fighting against Israel on the scale that Hezbollah had attacked Israel. Hamas could have easily declared war with the verdict it gained in the elections where its campaign was focused mainly on eliminating Israel from the region. It was also an indication that when even militants are elected they could temper their extremist ideology in order not to lose popular support. Suppression of democracy also has a tendency to encourage radical outfits. In Egypt, the good showing of the Brotherhood in December's (2006) election was a salutary warning to the eternally ruling Hosni Mubarak that it is not such a clever idea to keep locking up your liberal opponents. Where Islamists do well, it is often because they are the only opposition left standing.[22]

The long slumbering outcry against modernity has gained a foothold in Islamic countries. For reasons good or bad, Islam is the cynosure of all political, cultural and social turmoil. Control of men and women in the name of religion has its own flavour of keeping a society from making any sort of economic progress. It is an uncovered fact of everyday part of living in the Middle East that people, in that domain of the world, are regressed through censorship, state edicts, intellectual submission and medieval punishments with the blessing of religious hands in all political, social, and economic decisions.

---

20. ibid
21. *The Economist*, The one thing Bush got right, 4th February, 2006, p. 9
22. ibid

Democracy is an irrelevance for Islamic fundamentalists. It stares ungainly at its ideological concept of 'God's rule'. For them, to embrace democracy is akin to poison the rule of God. Radical Islamists believe and avow that God alone has the power to make laws while those mortal souls making laws can only be apostates. This idea finds a ready embrace only among a 'minority' while the rest of the Islamic world would be happy to have democratic governance if only they could be provided with one. Therefore, the argument that political Islam is rooted in rigidity and that it is incompatible with democratic values does not hold water. The incompatibility of Islam with democracy is an excuse, a ploy and a bluff put forth by those vested-interests in the upkeep of religious dominance over politics. The fact that democracy has taken root in Turkey, Indonesia, Morocco, and Bangladesh, however flawed the democratic system in those countries, goes to show that Islam is compatible with democracy. Democracy cannot heal a society steeped in ancient conflicts, archaic institutions, and antediluvian ideas but a sure step towards democracy can create civic institutions and modernize stagnant societies.

Free speech and Islam

When the Danish newspaper *Jyllands-Posten* published a cartoon of Prophet Mohammad caricaturing him with a bomb in his turban it was only a matter of time before frenzied protests around the Muslim world were going to erupt. It was clearly an act that was surely going to test the limits of Muslims' patience. The distasteful caricature of Prophet Mohammad further stirred a smouldering discontent that had already been brewing between the West and the Islamic world. The publication of the cartoon of Prophet Mohammad came at a time when Islam had been under challenge from radical Islamists and terrorists who readily hijack the religion to fulfil their political and ideological ambitions. Roughly two decades ago, political relations between Europe and the Islamic world were strained by the publication of Salman Rushdie's book The Satanic Verses. Sadly once again the relations were tested by the cartoon episode. The protests against the cartoon also highlighted how differently 'freedom of expression' is taken in the West and treated in the Islamic world.

The radicalization of Islam and absence of secularism in Muslim states have succoured the revival of fundamentalist forces. The cartoons, surely, were not in good taste. The insulting images of Prophet Mohammad came at the time when three biggest flashpoints of tussle between the West and Islam were going on in the world—the illegal detention of prisoners at Guantanamo Bay, invasion of Iraq by the Allied forces, and widespread suspicion of Muslims living in the West after the 9/11 terrorist event.

Regardless of all the rhetoric calling for tolerance, the divide between Islam and the West remains as testy as ever but a few notches higher in the last decade or so. The cartoon episode generated waves of protests in Afghanistan, Syria, Lebanon, Indonesia, and Iran which included attacks on Western embassies. Sermons were blared out by splenetic Imams fulminating against the insult to the faith. There were also calls soliciting Osama bin Laden to 'punish' the West. Iran and several other Middle Eastern countries boycotted Danish consumer products. Fiery demonstrators burned Danish flags to douse their wrathful ire. The hysterical protests flooded out of the passion with which Muslims identify themselves with their religion.

The offence taken by Muslims was understandable but the peculiarity of protestations including the smashing of buildings, damaging public properties, banning food imports, countries recalling their Ambassadors and the resulting loss of lives showed an utter lack of democratic decorum in expressing their anger and frustration. As the leading article in The Times put it, "Muslims ... have a right to protest about the cartoons and, if they want, to boycott the publications concerned. To move from there to holding ministers responsible for the editorial decisions of a free press in their nations, to urge that all products from a country be ostracized or, worse still, to engage in violence against people or property is to leave the field of legitimate complaint and enter one of censorship enforced under threat of intimidation. That free speech is misunderstood in much of the Islamic realm shows how much progress has yet to be made."[23]

If freedom of speech is a rarity in Islamic countries, the reaction in Britain and America, long considered the bastions of democracy, was knee-jerk to muffle free speech. Freedom of speech is clearly tested when religious sensitivity gets ruffled. As soon as the protests over the cartoon broke out, leaders in some Western countries swiftly marched to denounce the cartoons as unacceptable and promptly put the lid of injunction on several newspapers from publishing the cartoons. The road to tyranny of gag order starts from a little step. Britain's foreign secretary Jack Straw called the publication of cartoons "insulting", "insensitive", "disrespectful", and "wrong."[24] The US government later described the cartoons as "offensive to the beliefs of Muslims and criticized the European press." The statements of both British and US governments were right for denouncing the despicability of the cartoon but the action to curb the publica-

---

23. *The Times*, Leading article, Drawing the line, 3rd February, 2006

24. *The Guardian*, Cartoon controversy spreads throughout the Muslim world, 4th February, 2006, http://www.guardian.co.uk

tion of these cartoons ran in the face of a democratic culture that both countries have long carried in their bosom with pride. It was no surprise that the two governments, US and Britain, who were the forerunners in destabilizing Muslim heartland with their belligerent armies, stamping their authority in Afghanistan, in the ousting of Saddam Hussein, had to kiss and make up with the Muslims.

Communal clashes and religious intolerance often stem out of misunderstanding and misinformation. Misunderstanding and misinformation grow out of suppression of information and interaction. Enlightenment never dawns on a society willing and ready to squelch criticism and free speech. By controlling freedom of expression due to a fear of clash of civilization is to silently fuel simmering discontent among people over 'misunderstood' and 'misinformed' parts of religion or of their community. People who feel they are prevented in voicing or opining their ideas and feelings about terrorism, global issues and religion will only start to hate their fellow humans who may have a different value-system to theirs. Where people speak out, assess opinions and co-exist without fear or violence or political repercussion democracy assumes greater significance. Encouraging people to speak out and "... spreading and strengthening" the values of free expression can possibly bring "... best hopes for avoiding the incomprehension which can lead civilizations into conflict."[25]

Charges against democracy

Democracy constantly faces challenges from a cross-section of critics for a number of reasons. Absence of secrecy and procedural delays are often cited as its weaknesses. There are also other criticisms, which form the core of charges against democracy—that it is a reservoir of ignorance; that party politics creates more divisions; that the tyranny of the majority prevails; and that it venerates incompetence. It is, therefore, imperative to look at each of the above four criticisms with clarity and refute them tooth and nail.

Where ignorance rules

Two views prevail regarding popular ignorance occupying the centre stage of democracy. The first view is the election of ignorant men to positions of authority by a majority. The second view is the usurpation of power by few intelligent people over a majority of ignorant voters by manufacturing political consent through promises and rhetoric.

---

25. *The Economist*, Cartoon wars, 9th Feb, 2006 http://www.economist.com

The unending fervour to point to the existent 'ignorance' inbred in democracy has always been a fad among critics of democracy. In truth, ignorance shadows every political system. As interesting as it may sound to suggest that politicians need to be trained just as a doctor, an architect or an artist is trained in his respective field, such arguments abound as if managing unknown and unknowable desires and aspirations of millions, or a billion people was easy. Indeed, as easy as learning a subject relatively limited in scope that is based on formulae, or a few rules, or experiments or practice of an art, or a skill or a monotonous job. If democracy is so weakened by the claim of the rule of the ignorant, then communist Cuba, where democracy is seen as an unwelcome disease by Fidel Castro, must be free of ignorance and flying high on the magic carpet of economic prosperity. The country is notorious for torture, political imprisonment, control of the media, and forced exile of political dissidents.

The strength of democracy is its honest acceptance of human ignorance and limited knowledge. It is impossible for any human mind to comprehend the infinite variety of needs of people which compete for available resources and to attach a definitive value for each need, then rank each need in order of priority. The point which is so important is the basic fact that it is impossible for any man to survey more than a limited field, to be aware of the urgency of more than a limited number of needs. Whether his interests centre round his own physical needs, or whether he takes a warm interest in the welfare of every human being he knows, the ends about which he can be concerned will always be only an infinitesimal fraction of the needs of all men.[26] Democracy, without reservation, recognizes the limitations of the powers of human imagination and that it is impractical to grasp anything beyond the microscopic grain of the needs of all men which is why democracy functions through debate in formulating policies and presenting them to the public to accept or reject. The possibility of an ignoramus becoming a leader in a democracy is as strong as the likelihood of it in an undemocratic regime. The luxury for people in a democracy is the availability of the right to get rid of an 'ignoramus' peacefully through ballot without having to bite the bullet.

For Noam Chomsky it is not about the 'ignorant' leading a government. It is about 'intelligent' men making a life out of the "ignorance" and "superstition" of the masses. In his Mellon Lecture,[27] Chomsky quotes Harold Lasswell, a political

---

26. Friedrich A Hayek, *The Road to Serfdom*, (London, Routledge, 2001), p. 62
27. Noam Chomsky, *Democracy and Education*, Mellon Lecture, Loyola University, Chicago, October 19, 1994, http://www.smo.uhi.ac.uk/d3/chomsky.html

scientist, on the ignorance and superstition of the masses and the manipulation of modern techniques of propaganda to keep the public in line. He also asserts that "… it is the politically active segments of the population, the more educated and privileged, who are of prime concern. This is obvious in the United States, where the poor tend not even to vote, and more significant forms of political participation—the design and formulation of political programs, candidate selection, the requisite material support, educational efforts or propaganda—are the domain of the relatively narrow privileged elites."[28]

In one single sweep, the people are collectively dismissed as ignorant and incapable of sound political decisions. Unfortunately, Chomsky not only bases his opinion on America but fails to look at the case of India, the world's largest democracy housing a sizeable number of poor and illiterates, and who form the largest chunk of voters and regularly queue weathering the climate to eagerly cast their votes for the parties that speak their voice. In India it is the rich and the upper middle class communities that care less about casting their votes—quite in contrast to the poor. The underlining truth is that when an 'ignorant' party or leader assumes power in a democracy, there is always an option for the electorate to exonerate a non-performing entity without coup or bloodshed or revolution. When people are deemed ignorant and that they do not have the capability to choose their leaders, it is to prepare ground fertile for authoritarianism by taking away that important tool of voice—election. People need not be intelligent to resign themselves to the study of politics and economics before electing their leaders. People need basic rights and protection to speak their mind when their livelihood is threatened.

Evils of party politics

Is it true that party politics promote sectarian outlook? Is it true that party politics divides people into hostile camps pitting one against the other? Is it true that political leaders mould honey-coated policies to appeal to their clan or tribes? The firm reply to these questions is how one sees the workings of party politics. There is probably a pinch of truth in each of the questions above but to brush them aside as totally unnecessary to administer a society is to trample upon the interests of many for the narrow purposes of the ruling elite. Political parties may be sectarian when it comes to promoting the ideologies of their parties but they cause less injury provided there is respect for rule of law and that they do not unequivocally seek to establish their own ideologies to the exclusion of others.

---

28. Noam Chomsky, *Noam Chomsky Reader*, p. 132

Party politics may divide people into hostile camps but so long as such divisions bring forth a diversity of ideas they can only be beneficial to a country in the long-run. Leaders communicating to their constituencies with appealing words to convince the voters to accept policies which they regard are for wider benefit is better than authoritarians forcing their own agenda on the lives of people.

Political parties in democracies usually promote, but do not force, their own ideology. As societies become more diverse, the gravity of the significance of representing various communities, religions or ethnicities to bring them all together on a common national cause by respecting their private identities cannot be stressed enough. India, under the predominant rule of congress for about five decades, only made the differences of language and culture between various states starkly divided.

It is only the recent emergence of various regional political parties that has brought the hitherto non-represented as well as under-represented fringe groups at the forefront of national polity. In the 2004 Indian general elections, according to the Indian Elections[29] statistical information, a staggering 220 parties and 5,398 candidates (out of which 2,369 were independent ones) contested 543 seats for the Lower House of the Parliament while nearly 390 million voters cast their votes. Indian elections—considered the most complex and cumbersome in the world—apart from its ability to provide 'operations management' skills for those involved in organizing them is truly a matter meriting applause that any person who feels an issue so dear to his heart or to his people is free to take up the cause and present his 'proclamation' to the public to decide its acceptance in the ballot box. It is not an evil to take to the public a proposal that an individual feels important. It is rather an opportunity to bring to the public platform a reason to discuss and assess the weight of that reason.

Tyranny of majority

Defined as a phenomenon characterized by a sameness of majority public opinion that continually block a minority group's own interests, democracy is disparaged as representative of the tyranny of majority. It would indeed be a bad development should certain people, on account of the strength of their numbers, rule and dominate those who do not make up sufficient numbers to make their concerns heard by the government. But is tyranny of majority destroying democratic societies? Is majority blindly taken to contain more wisdom based purely on the

---

29. Indian Elections, *Election 2004 Facts and Figures*, http://
www.indian-elections.com/facts-figures.html

size of numbers? Does democracy, through its tyranny of majority, force weaker sections of society to yield to the majority? The answer to the questions above depends on whether 'minority' groups in a society are allowed recourse to justice should there be a violation of their rights or their interests mindlessly or deliberately crushed by those in power and those who make up their presence felt through their strength.

When India drew its marathon constitution in 1950 the principal exercise was to attend to a wide range of issues affecting those in the minority and unprivileged as well as underprivileged categories through centuries of casteism and social discrimination. The constitution of India unreservedly and emphatically delineates "... the cultural rights of minorities; the funding of minority educational institutions; the cultural rights of indigenous peoples; linguistic rights; the self-government rights of culturally distinct groups; asymmetrical federalism; legal pluralism; affirmative action for marginalized groups.[30]

Indian democracy in practice may not be as close to perfection as Sweden's but the survival of democracy in a country with innumerable differences and pluralities speaks of the protection several minorities—forming linguistic, religious, caste-based, economically-deprived, regional groups—enjoy with utter faith in judiciary and other democratic institutions. India has had its occasional share of mob-driven violence but the country's belief in the democratic values has long been its strength. Several concerns relating to minority interests have always been part of official state policy such as granting public holidays in order to bestow official recognition to minority religions; freedom in dress codes; the sensitivity in the history and teaching of India's multi-faceted cultures and traditions of minorities, and the commitment of government to fund minority religious practices and places of worship.

In contrast to Indian democracy, consider the status of minorities in Malaysia where the country is run by a government through its constitutional monarchy. Celebrating its 50th birthday in 2007 after gaining independence from Britain, the country is far away from its racial and religious tensions. As ethnic Chinese and Indians came to dominate the business and professions respectively it intensified the anxiety of native Malays of becoming marginalized in their own land. Instead of upping their competitive spirit the indigenous Malays have facilitated a clause in the constitution providing them with a share in employment, education and business.

---

30. Open Democracy, Rajeev Bhargava, *India's model: faith, secularism and democracy*, 3rd November, 2004, http://www.opendemocracy.net

At (the time of Malaysia's) independence, a "social contract" was struck in which the Indians and Chinese got citizenship while the indigenous peoples received privileged access to state jobs and education. After the 1969 riots, a far-reaching positive-discrimination policy was introduced, with the aim of increasing the indigenous groups' share of business ownership from just 4 percent to 30 percent.[31] The supporters of this discriminatory policy justify that it has kept peace in the country but it is threatening to stall the economic progress the country has made economically. The failure of Proton, a car maker, once a symbol of the country's economic ascendancy now has become emblematic of the country's inner travails. Malaysia is an apt specimen of 'tyranny of majority' where half the country's Malay populace exploit the minorities through an open policy of positive-discrimination. Such gross preferential and differential treatment of citizens would be criminal in a democratic society. Tyranny of majority is not what happens in an equality-committed Indian democracy but in a highly-flawed, constitutionally-discriminatory farcical democracy of Malaysia.

Veneration of incompetence

George Bernard Shaw once said that "democracy substitutes election by the incompetent many for appointment by the corrupt few." Democracy is often berated for sustaining administration run by less intelligent and immature men who, when assigned with the responsibility of the highest offices, are incapable of discharging their duties and responsibilities ably. Such an accusation may be true in the case of George W. Bush, or in a few cases. But to cite such exceptions as representative of a universal truth is to undercut and disregard the spectacular progress democratic nations, for instance the Scandinavian countries, have made over the years.

Competence is not a privilege of the very few. Managing a country in today's complex-ridden world of international markets, financial inter-dependency, endless movement of people between geographical borders, convergence of different cultures, the impact of evolving technologies and global politics, the call for maximization of democracy has never been more significant.

When SARS outbreak imperilled global stability, one country stood out in the midst for its authoritarian and incompetent governance—China. Doubtless, China in the last two decades has changed beyond imagination. In spite of its glittering skyscrapers, modern factories, and a growing band of globetrotting

---

31. *The Economist*, Putting the malaise into Malaysia, 2nd December, 2006, p. 65

well-educated Chinese, the country still is soaked heavily under the weight of its old authoritarian system. Fear of losing foreign investment, of endangering business opportunities and a blind assumption that SARS would die away as silently as it broke out, the Communist regime in China suppressed the seriousness of SARS until it went out of control and stirred up global suspicion on Chinese administration and its truthfulness.

Everyone can see that democracy isn't just a luxury. They can see that authoritarianism doesn't even guarantee stability. A government that represses information not only kills its people—and those of other countries—but it spreads panic and disbelief as its credibility erodes.[32] Despite its limitations, democracy is more than capable of making ordinary men capable in handling crises. The permissive role of political and civil rights through public debates and discussions demonstrably helps in averting disasters.

It would be quite pertinent in concluding this part with a comment from a reader in Beijing about an article which highlighted China's Communist Party's position that the "*laobaixing*—the common folk—are better off not knowing too much"[33] on Business Week over China's handling of SARS. The reader wrote: If we look back into history, we can find many ill results of this wrong position. These bad results can be avoided only if the people and the media express their views freely. We are delighted to see that top Chinese officials finally admit to incompetence in dealing with SARS. And we hope that this about-face is the herald of a new era of press freedom and continuing opening in China, not for foreign investment, but for the truth." [34]

When an individual or groups of 'elitist' individuals deem themselves to be the 'be-all' and 'end-all' of a nation's destiny, the spell of doom is bound to blanket its people in a pall of gloom. Detriment sprouts from an 'unshakable' belief in the infallibility of one's knowledge to manage the lives of people and resources of a country. We progress on the basis of the acceptance of the truth that human intelligence is relative, not absolute and a group of debating individuals, however

---

32. *Business Week Online*, China's deadliest plague: Authoritarianism, 18th April, 2003, http://www.businessweek.com

33. *Business Week*, SARS: An amazing about-face in Beijing, 5th May, 2003, http://www.businessweek.com

34. Peihong Yang, *Business Week Online*, International—Readers Report, 26th May, 2003, http://www.businessweek.com/magazine/content/03_21/c3834156_mz030.htm

mediocre in intelligence but knowledgeable in their experience to talk about the matters that affect them, is what makes a democratic society progressive.

CHAPTER 3

▼

THE SPECTRE OF TERROR

It lacerates life out of man, woman and child alike. It cripples your body as fear psychosis creeps into your mind. It alarms you at home, at office or on the street. It frightens you with its cold savage touch and sends shivers down your spine. It respects no human values. It cares for neither human rights, nor human lives. It knows no geographical boundaries. It knows no political decorum. It is devoid of common sense. Welcome to humanity's primitive instinct blanketed in the veil of legitimate struggle—terrorism.

Terrorism takes form when an individual or a group of individuals, wedded to a particular cause, goal or mission, promotes its political, religious or ideological goals through intimidation of public or government by resorting to means that are both violent in nature and unconventional in execution. Thriving through inculcation of fear among the public at large, resorting to indiscriminate killing of civilians and shunning of all rational approach to problems, terrorism wilfully violates all forms of legitimate protest to get its message across and to accomplish its purpose.

Terrorists prefer labelling themselves as revolutionaries who are intent on bringing about radically different changes to established norms of society. When people rise as a single force to overthrow or thoroughly replace an established government or political system it amounts to revolution. Where a revolution, at least in theory, should exempt civilians from indifferent murder and killing, terrorism works exactly in the opposite fashion.

Therefore, equating 'terrorism' with 'revolution' is to deliberately ignore the way terrorism approaches a problem or an issue that a 'revolution' does not. No protest that takes to wholesale murder of civilians for no fault of theirs would ever deserve the label of 'revolution'. No civilized society condones a free license to terrorize itself or to live in a climate of fear and uncertainty. This is where terrorism assumes its despicable image, for it denies human life, human dignity, human rights, and human liberty.

For the terrorist, the word 'terrorism' may be a misnomer.[1] A terrorist habitually identifies himself as a liberator, a rebel or a freedom fighter. An Osama bin Laden sees himself as a liberator of all Muslims from the 'contamination' of non-Muslims, infidels, and idol-worshippers; a Shamil Basayev, the Chechen leader, sees himself a rebel fighting the Russians; a member of LTTE (Liberation Tigers of the Tamil Eelam) regards himself as a freedom fighter struggling for his community's independence from the government. There are scores of other terrorists who anoint themselves as revolutionaries, militants, strugglers or martyrs as the terms become muddled in a puddle of semantic ambiguity. The common string uniting these individuals, or groups, is their indifference to the killing of civilians to pursue their goal.

Never before has the world spoken in single voice to tackle a universal challenge as gripping and complicated as tackling the cancer of terrorism. Terrorism is not a new phenomenon. The world saw it yesterday; is seeing it today and will, doubtless, be seeing it tomorrow. Spanning at least 2,000 years, terrorism, from time to time, reared its ugly head at various stages in the history of human existence. Around 66–70 AD, the Zealots, a group of Jewish political activists, persisted with a staunch terrorist campaign to oust the Roman Empire. In the 11th century, a radical Islamic sect known as Hash-Ishiim used to drug their victims and murder anyone for a cause they believed to be righteous. Between the 11th and 14th centuries the Crusades in their attempt to recapture the Holy Land (Palestine) assaulted civilian Muslims. The French Revolution during the 18th century had its own period of 'Reign of Terror' licensing the extensive use of guillotine to decapitate any person seen as an enemy or a conspirator. In modern times, we have seen the Anarchists such as Mikhail Bakunin, the Irish Republican Army, the Islamic radicals such as the Hamas, the Hezbollah and hardcore terrorist outfits such as the al-Qaeda.

---

1. David J. Whittaker, *Terrorism: Understanding the Global Threat*, (London, Longman, 2002), p. 12

Impregnated with intolerance and prejudice, and convinced of the 'rationale' and 'righteousness' of their ideology—howsoever deranged they are—terrorists find it practically hard to acquire power through democratic means. In spite of their avowed political cause or religious mission or ideological objective, terrorism has hardly ever won popular support for its philosophy of violence apart from a like-minded minority few. Terrorism has, surely, spread its deadly tentacles across the length and the breadth of the universe through its rationale of intimidation and fear.

In the last two decades or so, terrorists have increasingly dotted the world with the gory taint of their beastly terror—Turkey, Indonesia, Iraq, Saudi Arabia, America, Britain, India, Pakistan, Afghanistan, and Sri Lanka are some of the places that bore their brutal brunt. Ever since terrorism came into existence, its soul has remained the same. It is just that only its *modus operandi* has changed.

Terrorism, of late, has assumed several avatars—through which it could unleash destruction, such as using chemical and biological weapons, suicide bombing, plane hijacking, or holding school children hostage. The flexibility of terrorists has given way to innovative methods of extreme violence. Modern day terrorists do not solely rely on 'weapons of mass destruction'. The spectacular bombing of World Trade Center in New York made one wonder if an aircraft could in fact be classed as a 'weapon of mass destruction.'

It was an indication of the willingness, adaptability, and ingenuity of terrorists to use any available tool or instrument to fulfil their hideous ambition. Whether it is an unsuspected London bomber with a rucksack on a public bus or a dodgy shoe-bomber in an aircraft or an innocent-looking fundamentalist planting a bomb in the suburban trains of Mumbai, the evolution of terrorism has become a truly grisly reality of vicious innovativeness!

The old game of terror now has innovated new tactics. Terrorism has undergone a paradigm shift. Gone are the days when terrorists were selective of their targets—the assassinations of French President Sadi Carnot in 1894, the stabbing of Austrian Empress Elizabeth in 1897 as well as the killing of Spanish Prime Minister Antonio Cánovas, India's Prime Ministers Indira Gandhi and Rajiv Gandhi—stand witness to how civilians were spared from terrorists' murderous frenzy. In the past, the victims were selected. At present, the killing has shifted from 'selective' to 'indiscriminate'. As security tightened and vigilance increased, the freedom with which terrorists targeted their victims so easily in the past has narrowed or has started to pose higher risk to their operations. The environment under which they operate, has thus forced them to look for an easy fodder—

unarmed and unsuspecting civilians—upon whom they can descend with an utter lack of human sensitivity.

Islam and its struggle

Religion has always been anathema to universal peace, especially when it has come under the purview of fundamentalists, extremists and fanatics, not to mention the ideologues. Despite all its claims to be the indispensable facet of life that brings supernatural comforts to the unhappy, the suffering, the bereaved, the old; that confers meaning and dignity upon the lowliest existence; that unifies people belonging to various hues and colours, religion has largely been responsible for many a war in human history or it has been exploited as a tool to settle political scores and create social fissures.

Religion is often extolled to have been a great force for forging unity among people. Often the unity forged by religion has only been parochial in nature always pitting one religious group against another. Mastering the art of nurturing tribal instincts among their adherents religions tend to encamp people into dividing themselves as 'us' versus 'them'. The unity promoted by religion has always been prejudiced at best and sectarian at worst. Such parochial unity has only aggravated intolerance in the society. If (such) unity leads to intolerance towards others, the consequences may be discrimination, persecution and even violent action.[2]

Nowhere is this bigoted unity more pronounced than in Islam. Apart from political or economic reasons for which people resort to bloody violence, modern day turbulence in the form of terrorism disproportionately falls on radical Islamism. Wherever a terrorist blitzkrieg erupts, rightly or wrongly, directly or indirectly, partially or wholly, Islamic anger, unfortunately, has a pinch of share in it, or so it seems. It is unfortunate that terrorism is more marked in places where the major religion is that of Islam.[3]

Entrenched so deeply in its own strictures of rigidity Islam struggles to adapt itself to changing times; to accept the evolving morals of the universe; to admit the growing multiplicity of numerous faiths. As a forlorn child struggling to find identity and in need of guardianship, Islam is trapped in an identity crisis. Islam, unfortunately, has come to be interpreted in various tones—from being a moderate religion to a violent faith. Several care-takers including militant guardians have carried it in their arms and have moulded it in their own perception. Islam

2. ibid, p. 92
3. ibid, p. 93

today stands hijacked in the radical wings of few extremists, fundamentalists, and terrorists as they frenetically promote their own interests—all in the name of protecting or spreading the virtues of Islam.

The unhappiness of Islamic fundamentalism springs from its discomfiting relationship with the modern world. It is rooted in its despising of any culture which it adjudges un-Islamic specifically the ones impressed with western values. It sees "… western culture as materialistic, corrupt, decadent, and immoral."[4] Islamism finds modern living, particularly western values, as a threat to its own faith, culture, and ideology. It is a rattling contention between values encompassing secularism and ideologies impregnated with religious radicalism. Secularism excludes religious interests away from civil affairs and public education in utter contrast to religious fundamentalism which endeavours to take charge of every aspect of both personal and public affairs of individuals.

As for radical Islam, secularism is incompatible for two reasons: 1) the rule of Shari'ah is compulsory, the basic laws and regulations of which are not changeable. Since such laws and regulations describe not just acts of worship and also the relationship between men and women and other practices of conducting one's life; and 2) secularism in Islam is clear unbelief (Kufr) as secularism separates the place of religion in civil and political affairs it goes against the tenets of Islam. While traces of secularism can be found in modern Islamic countries such as Turkey and Malaysia, which prove that secularism is indeed compatible with Islam if it is allowed to function, where faiths other than Islam are allowed to flourish, accommodation of other faiths in the Muslim world, by and large, is quite conspicuous by its absence.

It is a fact that several non-Muslims living in Muslim countries do not even have the liberty to practice their faith. In several Islamic countries basic religious rights are crushed under several pretexts differing both in scope and degree. For instance, the violation of religious rights "… ranges from Saudi Arabia's ban on non-Muslim worship to the more subtle pressure on the Copts of Egypt who fear the rising power of Islamism. In divided lands like Nigeria and Sudan, Christians and 30,000 Jews report harassment, discrimination and hostile propaganda from the official media; followers of Baha'i faith suffer even more."[5]

Fundamentalism, when ingrained with intolerance, renders itself incapable of any agreement and compromise with values that differ sharply from its own. It is

---

4. Samuel Huntington, *The Clash of Civilizations and the Remaking of World Order*, (London, Touchstone/Simon & Schuster, 1998), p. 213

5. *The Economist*, Muslims and the pope, 2nd December, 2006, p. 13

something that is in harmony with fundamentalist-Islam. Fundamentalist-Islam stubbornly underpins the beliefs that:

- An inner 'voice of God' requires unquestioning obedience and fanatical devotion.

- The code of Koran and the rigid Shari'ah code of conduct are to be observed so strictly that unbelievers, infidels, or followers of the Great Satan are to be rejected and conquered. Their destruction becomes a sacred duty and a crusade.

- The Will of God and the doctrine of Koran make our actions legitimate, however unrestrained and violent they may be.

- Our leaders in belief (or in the field) will be given undying respect and loyalty.

- Failure to carry out a mission or to be tempted by heresy is unpardonable.

- The faithful will receive final reward but only if they remain absolutely steadfast.[6]

String these beliefs together against the western concept of individualism as being independent of religion; against the economic backwardness into which several Islamic nations are ensnared and against the political cauldron between an Islamic society and a non-Islamic one—it incubates a tinder-box of bloodthirsty passions just waiting to explode.

No other terrorist group represents more tellingly than al-Qaeda for all its deep-rooted fanaticism, ferocious fundamentalism, ruthless extremism, and violent radicalism together with its globally-spread network of terror cells. The organisation is notorious for its regular terrorist attacks the world over including the World Trade Center attacks, bomb blasts in Kenya and Tanzania and a host of other terrorist crimes across Asia and Europe. Just before al-Qaeda reached the pinnacle of its worldwide notoriety, it found a patronizing sanctuary in Afghanistan under the Taliban. It turned out to be a perfect marriage between a fundamentalism-driven 'terrorist' organisation, al-Qaeda, and a fundamentalism-oriented 'political' outfit, Taliban.

While al-Qaeda, under the patronage of Osama bin Laden, provided financial and military support to the Taliban the latter protected the terrorist organisation

---

6. David J. Whittaker, p. 96

with political security. It was a toxic blend of religion and politics at its deadly zenith directed at ridding Islam from the 'fangs' of western influence. To establish a sterile, puritan and chaste society, Taliban decreed against debate, gambling, music, videos, television, kite-flying, education of women, curfew on mobility of women and their dress while dissent was vehemently stamped down. Even men's beard was not spared if it did not meet the required length. Taliban created a Ministry of Vice and Virtue to upkeep morals of Islam on the straightest of lines. If any individual violated the religious codes set out by the Ministry of Vice and Virtue, the government's Religious Police would deal with it by meting out punishments to 'law-breakers'.

Although the Taliban did not carry out any terrorist attack it provided the ultimate haven for Osama bin Laden and his al-Qaeda operatives for executing terrorist operations worldwide. Similar strains at varying degrees are also found in Afghanistan's neighbour Pakistan where voices of Islamic fundamentalism screech through the country's corridors calling for extermination of both imagined as well as perceived threats arising out of 'opponents' of Islam and liberal-minded Muslims.

Wilting under the global phenomenon of insecurity emanating out of a stigma of suspicion shadowing Muslims in the non-Muslim dominated parts of the world has bred a feeling of isolationism among members of Islam. An impending fear that the future does not belong to them is indicative of the sense of insecurity they have to live with.

The biggest thorn in the world afflicting the relations between the West and Islam is the ongoing struggle between Israelis and Palestinians. No other issue has grabbed and united the entire Arab and Muslim world than the perceived suffering of the Palestinians. The seemingly endless crisis has prompted many in the Islamic world to think that the rest of the world has neither remorse nor support for the disadvantaged Palestinians shackled in a losing war against Israel. Moreover, the global perception towards Muslims after the 9/11 incident and the ensuing 'war on terror' propelled them into an abiding wave of suspicion. Insecurity feeds vulnerability. The Palestine-Israel conflict has taken such deep roots in the psyche of Muslims around the world that every Islamic fundamentalist, authoritarian and terrorist organisation seeks legitimacy and a following and puts the agenda of the 'liberation' of Palestine at the forefront.

When requested to vacate Kuwait after invading during the Gulf War, Saddam Hussein asked the world, as a precondition, to make Israelis evacuate the West Bank and Gaza. Osama bin Laden justifies his acts of terror and killing of innocent civilians by making the Palestinian issue the most important cause for the Muslim world. While politically-driven militant organisations such as the Hamas, Hezbollah, and other Islamist *jihadists* all justify the murder of innocent Jews and violence to resolve the Arab-Israeli conflict. The struggle of Islam in a world that has changed radically and profoundly is certainly not finished yet as Islamic radicals are ever so focused to take the religion back to its days of glory.

Poverty and terrorism

Amidst a plethora of terrorist attacks and consequent efforts by world governments to tackle the recurring menace, there is a pervading talk about uprooting the 'cause' of terrorism. Often, the common refrain goes: 'remove poverty to eradicate terrorism' and a call for increased aid to poor countries to eliminate terrorism. Jeffrey Sachs argues that "... to fight terrorism we need to fight poverty and deprivation as well."[7] Michael Moore asserted that "... poverty in all its forms is the greatest single threat to peace, security, democracy, human rights and the environment."[8]

Frustration and lack of hope fed by poverty can spur disaffected people into taking out their sense of grievance on their richer, wealthier and healthier counterparts. Poverty is a condition of economic deprivation. As such, poverty creates an environment forlorn of hope and promise whereby disaffected and vulnerable individuals become willing candidates in the hands of brainwashing politicians and religious fanatics to go on suicidal and homicidal terrorist missions. If Afghanistan had not been poor it would not have provided a loophole for the Taliban to usurp power or for al-Qaeda to establish its abode in that country. Despite all the talk and argument about poverty contributing to terrorism this only substantiates the link between poverty and terrorism indirectly.

It seems undeniably obvious that terrorism thrives in poor countries where political instability, religious violence and social sectarianism are dominant forces. But to charge poverty as the 'main' or 'single' cause of terrorism is to overlook the toxic cocktail of politics and religion that underpin the scourge of terrorism. Terrorism is a complex conundrum trapped in the intricate vicissitudes of politics and religion. Often muddled in the muddy waters of conflicting passions, interests and ideologies of politics and religion, pinpointing poverty as the primary cause of terrorism is nothing more than a perfunctory exercise.

Just because terrorists, in general, hail from countries riven by poverty does not mean that poverty alone breeds terrorism. The umbilical cord between terror

---

7. Jeffrey Sachs, *The End of Poverty*, (London, Penguin, 2005), p. 215
8. BBC, *Poverty fuelling terrorism*, 22nd March, 2002, http://news.bbc.co.uk

ism and poverty is as subtle as it is weak. Terrorists, by and large, do not kill people or raze down buildings to make the people they claim to fight for richer or wealthier. Nor do they, while claiming to fight for their religion, avow for removal of poverty. For instance, Islamic terrorists seek for a path to paradise by killing 'infidels'. Religious terrorists are more often overwhelmed by fundamentalist ideology than they are moved by any compunction for the poor.

Mohammad Atta, the suicide pilot of American Airlines that happened to be the first plane to ram into the World Trade Center, was not just a leader of the 9/11 attacks. (He) was the son of a moneyed Egyptian lawyer and official, and those who knew him have described him as a class snob and snazzy dresser. Atta spent his last nine years living in Germany and in the U.S. While he may have been linked to activist groups in Egypt, there is nothing in his record that indicates that he was a committed political extremist or even deeply religious. Rather, there is significant evidence that he came to his fanatical beliefs in Hamburg—home to as many as 2,500 Islamic radicals in a community of some 80,000 Muslims. No long-time Islamist "sleeper" deposited from the East, he was shaped by the environment of extremist Islamic politics at a German technical university.[9]

It is not just Atta who was born into a family of privilege to have become a terrorist. There are multitudes of individuals hailing from educated and financially well-to-do families who are charmed into accepting as their bounden mission to create an Islamic caliphate—a world government under the strict tenets of Islam. The main hijackers of the aircrafts on 9/11 apart from Atta "… were well-educated children of privilege. None of them suffered first-hand economic privation or political oppression. Equally important, it is becoming clear that hundreds, if not thousands, of graduates of bin Laden's schools for terror are Muslims who have grown up and been educated in the United States and Europe."[10]

The terror plot cracked in London in 2006 to blow up a dozen planes bound for America involved not people driven to desperate poverty but by those individuals enamoured by a perverted idea of Islamic salvation from the fangs of West. Those arrested on suspicion of having links to bomb the planes were educated and certainly 'not' poor. All those who were taken for questioning were British citizens. Many were well educated and middle class. One was the son of a former Tory party agent, another was the son of an architect.[11] The comment in The

---

9. Adrian Karatnycky, *Under our very noses*, National Review, 5th November, 2001, Vol 53, Issue 21

10. ibid

11. *The Sunday Times*, Focus: Terror in the skies, 13th August, 2006

Sunday Times put it succinctly that poverty is not a good enough claim to be a force behind terrorism:

> These extremists are drawn both from our educated classes and the Muslim underclass. The first alienated group seems susceptible to radical recruiters on university campuses, the latter to firebrands they meet in mosques or in prison. There they are fed the lines that the West is evil and corrupt. They are urged to look at a culture of binge drinking, reckless hedonism, moral laxity and materialism. They see little of the advantages to our society of freedom of choice, of religion, of individualism and of equality. Nor is it good enough to claim that extremism is fostered by poverty. Although Pakistanis and Bangladeshis are struggling to do as well as some other second or third-generation immigrant groups, many of the recruits are from relatively privileged backgrounds. It is more a matter of a battle for minds rather than pockets. Add to this the internet, the finishing school of global terror, and a legal system that appears to be inflexible about deporting foreign *jihadists*, and you have the ingredients for an explosive clash of cultures.[12]

The LTTE (Liberation Tigers of Tamil Eelam) emerged as a result of Sri Lanka's discriminatory policy of 'divide and rule' in order to favour the majority Sinhalese. The LTTE, though it brought the issue of the plight of minority Tamils through armed resistance, regularly resorts to terror tactics out of its obdurate obsession to have a separate Tamil homeland in Sri Lanka and to remain its undisputed ruler. The IRA (Irish Republican Army) sprang up against Britain's political and military occupation of Ireland. ETA (Euskadi Ta Askatasuna) has long been fighting for a separate Basque country and its actions are influenced more by interests of politics than poverty. In the case of Kashmir, which is ripped apart in an endless orgy of violence, it is a political fight for a greater land share between Pakistan and India but has always assumed a religious flavour to it. In the instance of Chechnya, it is a struggle for Chechens against the Russians for a separate statehood. In addition to their demand for a separate statehood, Chechen groups seek to spread Islamic jihad to the Caucasus region, a cause that has attracted foreign Islamic militants, some of whom are believed to be Arab fighters linked to al Qaeda.[13] Organisations such as the LTTE, IRA and ETA have involved in politically-motivated armed-resistance while killing several leaders and civilians in the process.

---

12. *The Sunday Times*, The enemy within, 13th August, 2006
13. Audra K. Grant, *The MIPT Terrorism Annual 2004, National Memorial Institute for the Prevention of Terrorism*, 2005

Pigeon-holing every strain of terrorism as an effect of poverty is a wilful disregard of the contributory nature of politics and religion to terrorism. Although current international terrorism embodies elements that have long characterized terrorist violence over the decades—such as the broad struggles between elites and the underprivileged, between rich and poor nations, and between traditional and non-traditional power—the distinguishing aspect of the recent trend in terrorist group is the centrality of religion.[14]

To hope that terrorism could be tackled by removing poverty from the face of the earth is a mirage that shows promise only to distort its appearance as one approaches reality. If poverty is linked to terrorism then the occurrence of terrorist activities around the world must have declined in proportion to global reduction in poverty. If anything, the number of terrorist attacks seems to have only increased in the face of declining poverty. Africa, the poorest continent in the world produces a relatively lower number of terrorists as against relatively more prosperous regions in the Middle East or Afghanistan or Pakistan. Despite a vibrant economic growth of nearly 7 percent Pakistan is consensually endorsed to be the global haven for budding terrorists trained in its Madrassas (Islamic religious schools), which are widely seen as terror nurseries.

When the hijackers rammed two civilian planes into the World Trade Center in America their intention was not to make the Muslim world richer. Nor did they ever grieve that their societies were poor and backward. The opposite of it was probably a plausible reason. Engendering in themselves a wilful hatred of western individualism, capitalism and materialism the hijackers were probably driven to remain 'poorer' and 'Islamic' rather than strive to be 'richer' and 'secular'. Osama bin Laden, himself the heir to a Saudi billionaire is said to control "a fortune widely estimated at $300 million. That sum is large anywhere, but in Afghanistan ... it can command an empire."[15] He recruits estranged individuals to take on the western world, particularly America. His anger stems from his hatred of everything the West represents. He is more concerned about promoting an Islamic caliphate than eliminating poverty in the Islamic world, let alone global poverty.

---

14. ibid, p5

15. *Forbes*, The cost of being Osama bin Laden, 14th September, 2001, http://www.forbes.com

The obduracy of ideology

When fanatical adherence to ideology reaches stratospheric heights the rush to irrational behaviour attracts a profuse attendance from willing candidates prompting to take on their targets through acts of terror. Nowhere is such a cold-hearted ideology more conspicuous than in the realm of Islam today. Ideology is the negation of common sense. It is the denial of reason. It is the nullification of judiciousness. Since ideology is deeply premised on the inflexibility of a belief or faith or doctrine it provincially suppresses any opposition that dares confront its logic. The essence of ideology lies in its obsession of something to the exclusion of everything else.

Ideology in any form is deleteriously ruinous. It yields a closed system of thought, rather than a necessary openness to experience.[16] In the historic past, there was the ideological fanaticism of the Church between the fourth and sixteenth centuries. Through the rise of Adolf Hitler, Germany went through the ideological hatred of the Jews. The cold war had been a bitter ideological battle between forces of communism and capitalism. Every ideology, in history, had brought its own share of misery to people. During the Middle Ages the Church was responsible for its rule through tyranny, fear and murder; Adolf Hitler's ideology of the superiority of 'Aryan' race led him to commit the worst atrocities in human history; Mao Tse Tung's ideology of propelling China to a superpower status through massive steel production cost over thirty million lives; Taliban's ideology of imposing a sterile form of Islam brought misery to Afghans and eventually its downfall. Ideologies have always been a cancer of human civilization curbing independent inquiry and open debate.

It is ironic that despite their catastrophic tendencies, ideologies refuse to disappear. For a fact, the summit of current ideological frenzy is occupied by Islam. To put it differently, Islam stands hijacked by a minority of fundamentalist ideologues gripped by a perverted idea of achieving Muslim salvation from the pangs of 'crass materialism', 'selfish individualism', 'relentless capitalism' and 'sweeping commercialism' or what it sees as 'western immorality' through wholesale killing of masses. Encased in its own code of moral, political and social rules fundamentalist-Islam aims at the integration of all aspects of human life. This causes a direct conflict in places where those values challenge its principles.

---

16. Vernon Bogdanor, *Big questions in history*, (London, Vintage, 2006), Edited by Harriet Swain, p. 46

Hazed by the ambiguity of its verses, Islam exists with a touch of vulnerability to its image as a peaceful religion. It is a chink that provides the fundamentalists with the armour they so desperately need to wreak destruction on their perceived enemies. Muslim leaders often harangue tirelessly as to the nature of non-violence Islam stands for. Sadly, but truly, the construct of verses in Koran often provide fundamentalist ideologues to twist their meanings to their advantage. Just sample this: Hassan Nasrallah, the leader of Hezbollah, the Lebanese militant party fighting Israel, has the Koranic verse inscribed on his Hezbollah flag—"Prepare for them *whatever* forces you can muster."[17] By no measure such a verse could be sanely termed as an unambiguous call for 'non-violence'. Nor does such a phrase indubitably rule out recourse to 'violence'. The term 'whatever' denotes 'whatever' means one could gather to prepare oneself for one's enemy.

No matter what argument is put forward to define the image of Islam by its scholars or believers or practitioners, in the perception of the non-Islamic world Islam is seen to be the "… only cultural system (religion) that seems regularly to produce people like Osama bin Laden or the Taliban who reject modernity lock, stock and barrel"[18] as they use or misuse Islam in pursuit of their ideological missions.

The challenge with Islamist ideology lies in its obduracy of shaping an individual's personal, political, economic and social life in strict accordance with the precepts of Islam. As such, it constricts one's freedom and eventually takes on a totalitarian nature disallowing to conduct one's life as one likes. As with any ideology—economic or political that can be balefully shallow in scope—ideologically-charged Islamism has scaled such heights where fanaticism is filled with a readiness for extreme violence with utter absence of reason. Where such irrational ideology dominates rationality remains stunted while percept becomes blunted. Hassan Nasrallah himself had said that, "martyrdom is the best way of passing to the eternal world."[19] Having lost his eldest son in the 1997 war against Israel he went on to say: "I am sure that my son is in paradise with God Almighty"[20] as if he could see 'paradise' through a crystal ball.

The ideological obsession is not a new phenomenon forming the substratum of religious thinking. Christianity had been through the same ideological mess during the Middle Ages—an era when Islam was regarded as a fount of liberalism

---

17. Time, *The Chic Sheik*, 21st August, 2006
18. Francis Fukuyama, The Guardian, *The West has won*, 11th October, 2001
19. ibid
20. ibid

and modernism. What an irony! The tables have now been turned. The same ideology that divided men of individualism and men of faith has now come to divide the world between 'us' and 'them'. The maniacal belief in the unquestioning supremacy of one's own god has wedged humanity into believers and non-believers.

Every religion, even society, holds a certain percentage of fanatical ideologues. Some are relatively harmless while others become dangerously murderous when power subsumes with their uncompromising belief system. Osama bin Laden and his glorifiers squarely fall into the latter category. For they project themselves as the sole voice of their faith. Since the time bin Laden turned to '*jihad*', the actual meaning of which is often clouded by its double entendre, fundamentalism-driven Islam has taken a deadly twist. For the moderates '*jihad*' is a 'striving' for reward, blessing, prosperity, victory, and glory. There is nothing wrong in an individual striving in the way he does to shape his life in a way that he deems fit. But when the same *jihad* or striving becomes coloured by extremism it takes a whole new dimension to its stature. Thus *jihad* tends to become an unforgiving moralizing force keenly intent on speaking the only language it knows—the language of terror. '*Jihad*' then becomes a striving 'to kill those who worship other gods; who worship idols; who tread the path forbidden by Allah; or to instil terror into the hearts of the infidels'.

An individual's world-view in fact is shaped by the education he receives. The purpose of education is to bring out the hidden potential of an individual for his self-enhancement, the results of which thereby would enhance human welfare in general. Hence, education must be liberal, aim to promote tolerance and a critical learning of things as well as creative learning. Few societies are committed to providing a wholesome education to their subjects. Some societies have none of it. Some have less of it. Some construct a lot of their education in religious fundamentalism or extremism or radicalism. Unfortunately, some Madrassas, if not all, have come to be deemed to provide education with a fanatical flavour. The mushrooming of Madrassas dedicated to preaching Islam overlooks the diversity of the world and the importance of acceptance of differences. Madrassas are seen to provide food, shelter and education for many poor children. But for many a Madrassa, secularism is a form of apostasy.

Madrassas are turning out to be Jihadi factories, bent on churning out hardcore *jihadi* warriors who are singularly proficient on the 'ideological' accent with an instant readiness to assume terror roles, thriving under the garb of education promoting communitarian and religious values. In the face of globalization prompting countries to educate their citizens on honing their technical and educational skills and to have a wider world-view, the popularity of Madrassas in promoting a constricted view of the outside world has made giant strides. In Pakistan, there are about 12,000 Madrassas of which 7,000 are claimed to have been reformed. Still, that leaves "… 5,000 unreformed—presumably the problematic ones.[21] Bangladesh too has seen an escalation in the number of Madrassas within its borders. In 1970, there were 1,500 registered (Madrassas) with the government. Today there are nearly 8,000.[22]

The well-known notoriety of Madrassas rooted in Pakistan and the hitherto lesser known yet growing ones in Bangladesh where Madrassas are setting up their bases have few things in common—both countries have sizeable populations reeling under government neglect, administrative sloth and bureaucratic corruption propelling disaffected individuals to find comfort in radicalized ideology—a malignant colonization of mind as well as of thought leading to utter incapacitation of reason and rationality.

The war on terror

No sooner did two civilian aircrafts rammed into the World Trade Center in New York on the morning of 11th September 2001, in addition to the hijacking of two more passenger jet airliners on that same fateful day, killing scores of civilians than the rhetoric and the ensuing foolhardy adventures of 'war on terror' emerged. The phrase has achieved such a cultish status that any government in its fight against terrorism now uninhibitedly declares a 'war on terror' without even understanding its effectiveness, or to put it more tersely, its ineffectiveness.

The phrase 'war on terror' seems as bungled as its fight against terrorists who are spread out in unknown nooks and invisible crannies of the globe. Doubtless, terrorism is grave; it is worrying and it poses a real threat. But the 'war on terror' unfortunately has elicited more questions than it has provided any answers to the puzzle of terrorism.

America's 'war on terror' is a partial success in Afghanistan only to the extent that it dismantled Al-Qaeda, forced Osama bin Laden into hiding, and uprooted the Taliban from power and that it managed to hold elections in that country. Even though the country has an elected President the notorious opium-trade is still active and the remnants of Taliban are mounting a continual challenge to the

---

21. *The Economist*, The general at war, (Print Edition) 21st July, 2005, http://www.economist.com

22. BBC, *Bangladesh and Islamic militants*, 25th February, 2005, http://news.bbc.co.uk

government. Whatever success America gained in Afghanistan it soon squandered in its limited victory by the Iraqi misadventure.

Built around a web of lies, or perhaps on an exaggerated speculation that Saddam Hussein hid chemical and biological weapons and that he was seeking nuclear weapons to attack America, the case for 'war on terror' proved to be entirely flawed and false. The charges levelled by America and its allies were categorically baseless as it was they who, in the first place, created Saddam Hussein into the monster that he was to become later. (Way) back in the late 1950s, when Saddam consecrated his party membership by wielding a pistol in a botched assassination attempt against Iraq's then president, Abdul Karim Qasim, the Baath (a political party which Saddam later was to lead) was favoured by Western powers as a foil to both the powerful Iraqi Communist Party and to the pro-Russian Nasserists. The West welcomed the 1968 coup that brought Saddam into power. When he invaded revolutionary Iran in 1980, America and its allies helped quietly but generously with credits, arms and satellite intelligence. Later, they turned a blind eye to his use of chemical weapons, first against Iranian soldiers and then against his own unruly Kurds. Donald Rumsfeld paid the Iraqi leader a courtesy visit in 1983. For a time, the CIA helpfully contended that it was Iran, not Iraq, that had dumped poison gas on the Kurdish city of Halabja.[23]

Defying the UN advice, the US and Britain along with few other allies invaded Iraq but gathered neither any sign nor evidence of weapons of mass destruction. While no evidence emerged as to their wild claims, George Bush and Tony Blair unashamedly changed their original charge of Saddam Hussein hiding 'weapons of mass destruction' to removing his dictatorial regime for his 'crimes against humanity' and thereby bringing democracy to Iraq. The paradigm shift failed to cut ice with the general public in the West, let alone the Muslim world as America, together with its principal ally Britain, was seen to employ double standards in dealing with rogue regimes and terror states. America's continuing friendship with a quasi-dictatorial regime in Pakistan, its tolerance of Saudi Arabia where democracy does not even exist, its perceived weakness in confronting North Korea that openly seeks nuclear weapons and its perplexity in dealing with a belligerent Iran which also wants to become nuclear—all seem dubious when America talks of bringing democracy in parts of the world where freedom and liberty are suppressed.

So far, the 'war on terror' in Iraq remains an utter failure. This view is further bolstered by the statement of Gareth Evans, the President of International Crisis

---

23. *The Economist*, The blundering dictator, January 6th 2007, p. 42

Group when he said that "we are looking at Iraq's complete disintegration into failed-state chaos, threatening to drag down much of the region with it."[24] The 'war on terror' has made its inherent chinks more glaring; it has made the world more insecure; and it has put the world in a more precarious situation. While the 'war on terror' has foundered in its efforts to eliminate terrorists it has provided the *jihadists* with an opportunity to recruit more 'martyrs' to their cause. At least, that is what it looks like in Iraq where the country offers prospective martyrs and *jihadists* both training and a live arena to exhibit their terrorist credentials. Since invading Iraq in 2003, America and its allies are finding it ever more difficult to tame the chaos, mayhem and killing, ripping the country asunder day in and day out. Though the invasion has managed to impose a crude democracy on the country it has only widened the wedge between the Shias and the Sunnis. The status quo is only encouraging the recruitment of more *jihadists* intent on bombing and murdering everyone and anyone in sight. Even the execution of Saddam Hussein, who himself was largely an entity borne out of Western interests to interpret political trends in the Middle East, seems to have offered no let-up in the country's recurrent bombings and attacks.

Ever since America declared its 'war on terror' no significant success has ever been made in obliterating the ubiquitously spread terrorism, and the invisibly existing terrorists. If anything, terrorist activities have only increased around the world. According to the National Memorial Institute for the Prevention of Terrorism's (MIPT) annual report on terrorism, there is an increase in the frequency of global terrorist activity. The year 2001, which was also punctuated by the 9/11 attacks, saw a noticeable upswing in terrorist activity (1,732 incidents) from recent years. Global terrorism continued to gain momentum during 2002, against the backdrop of the launch of the U.S.-led war on terrorism, as violent activity was even more frequent (2,648) attacks than in the previous year. However, this pattern did not continue into 2003, which shows a modest decline in terrorist activity (1,897 attacks).[25] The year 2004 endured 2,647 incidents and 2005 recorded 4,962 incidents."[26] The year 2005 saw a mammoth increase in terror incidents by 86 percent from the previous year. The only year when terrorist incidents were lower compared to other years was in 2003. It was also the year

---

24. International Crisis Group, *After Baker-Hamilton: What to do in Iraq*, Media Release, 19th December 2006, http://www.crisisgroup.org

25. Audra K. Grant, The MIPT Terrorism Annual 2004

26. Terrorist Incident Reports. For more historical data and figures on terror incidents, injuries and fatalities, go to MIPT website, www.mipt.org

when the U.S invaded Iraq. Perhaps, it was a year when terrorists might have to gone to reassess and redraw their strategies to counter a wider presence of the American army.

The 'war on terror' is a campaign launched by the United States and its allies to end international terrorism by pre-emptively eliminating terrorists and discouraging states from sponsoring terrorists. Five years into its operation, the 'war on terror' has neither ended international terrorism nor the terrorist bombings the regularity of which have become a commonality rather than an exception. Going by the MIPT Terrorism Knowledge Base,[27] the year 2006, recorded a total of 6,425 terrorist incidents averaging just over 535 deaths per month and over 17 deaths per day at the hands of terrorists. It raises suspicion as well as the futility of the 'war on terror' as it appears to be fighting the shadows of terror, not terrorism itself. That is probably due to the fact that 'war on terror' fights terrorism in the same manner as a conventional war would be fought. Perchance, no realization has yet dawned on the proponents of 'war on terror' that War and Terrorism are two separate entities operating entirely differently.

The workings of both 'war' and 'terror' are diametrically opposed to each other. No matter how many armies and soldiers are employed to hunt the terrorists, the task will endlessly be prolonging. No army is ever going to destroy terror cells. Even if one cell is destroyed there will be several others mushrooming elsewhere. There are several reasons why armies will be inadequate in the fight against terrorism.

Terrorist cells are randomly and loosely networked. Armies are tightly regulated. Terrorists are segregated in various parts of the world. Armies are congregated in a specific location. Terrorists plan and attack at various locations. Armies are confined to a particular geographical area. Unlike traditional armies, guerrilla groups and terrorists do not ... hold territory."[28] Terrorists have polycentric leadership even though they have inspirational figureheads such as Osama bin laden or the late Abu Musab Al Zarqawi. Armies have a hierarchical leadership, hence command and instruction cascade top-down. Terrorists are driven by ideology

---

27. ibid, I have calculated the number of terrorist incidents that have occurred from the 1st of January 2006 to the 31st of December 2006 based on the monthly statistics provided by MIPT on its website in its Terrorist Incident Reports under MIPT Terrorism Knowledge Base, Incidents by Date section.

28. Lawrence Freedman, *Worlds in Collision—Terror and the Future of Global Order*, (Basingstoke/New York, 2002, Palgrave Macmillan), Edited by Ken Booth and Tim Dunne, p. 38

hence the lack of a command structure while Armies invade for national cause. Terrorists, by and large, are invisible or simply look civilian. Armies, or for that matter, the soldiers are visible, and uniformed.

Armies are bound by time and place. Terrorists are unbound by those very factors as they "… need time more than space, for it is their ability to endure while mounting regular attacks that enables them to grow while the enemy is drained of patience and credibility."[29] Armies communicate through structured channels. Terrorists communicate through unstructured or random communication channels. Armies direct their resources towards their targets. Terrorists utilize whatever available resources they have at their disposal to target whatever or whoever they want. Terrorist organizations are not strangers to fund-raising in the manner that political organisations and business institutions raise funds. Al-Qaeda, for instance, has always depended heavily on donations, and its global fundraising network is built upon a foundation of charities, non-governmental organisations, and other financial institutions that use websites and Internet-based chat rooms and forums. The fighters in the Russian breakaway Chechnya have likewise used the Internet to publicize the numbers of bank accounts to which sympathizers can contribute.[30] Armies are funded by governments under a pre-planned budget therefore they are limited by the sources through which they can raise finance for their war requirements. US President George Bush initiated the 'War on Terror' blindly hoping that America with its military might would be able to "… control all the crucial variables in a chaotic world situation."[31] But in utter contrast to expected returns on the 'war on terror', everyday world events prove uncontrollable and turbulent.

The global reach of communication technologies has armed those who aspire to wreak destruction on communities. Through the internet, these loosely interconnected groups (such as the Hamas and al-Qaeda) are able to maintain contact with one another—and with members of other terrorist groups. The Internet connects not only members of the same terrorist organizations but also members of different groups. For instance, dozens of sites supporting terrorism in the name of *jihad* permit terrorists in places as far-removed from one another as Chechnya and Malaysia to exchange ideas and practical information about how to build bombs, establish

29. ibid

30. Thomas Friedman, *The World is Flat*, (London, Penguin, 2006) p. 535

31. Immanuel Wallerstein, *Worlds in Collision—Terror and the Future of Global Order*, (Basingstoke/New York, 2002, Palgrave Macmillan), Edited by Ken Booth and Tim Dunne, p. 99

terror cells and carry out attacks.[32] It has helped them to expend few resources for a massive benefit to campaign their ideologies to a wide range of people around the world. Terrorists use the Internet not only to learn how to build bombs but also to plan and coordinate specific attacks. Al Qaeda operatives relied heavily on the Internet in planning and coordinating the September 11 attacks.[33]

Terrorists do not actually require sophisticated weapons to kill or terrorize people. Use of sophisticated weapons as well as accessibility to weapons of mass destruction is practically quite difficult especially in an integrated world. It is hard to imagine a terrorist confronting a Tomahawk missile with another equivalent missile. Terrorists are fully aware of their lack of resources as they are with their possessions. They largely depend on scooping freelance expertise (bomb makers, suicide bombers, combatants) into their fold through indoctrination. Terrorists use any tool or equipment or weapon which they deem usable depending on the conditions of supply of or accessibility to their weapons of choice at a particular time. It is also hard to invest in weapons or construct a weapons factory away from international vigilance. The 9/11 terrorists did not require any hi-tech equipment to ram the planes and to kill the passengers. It was such an extremely low-tech mission in which "the hijackers used their own names, public web terminals, frequent flier identifiers, and unencrypted e-mail messages to keep in touch."[34] The only strength in a terrorist arsenal is network-building to supply weapons, to recruit martyrs and spreading its ideology. A terrorist organisation survives so long as there is a steady supply of weapons, funds, and resources.

The brief yet relevant comparison highlighted above is an indication of how 'war on terror' cannot actually win over terrorism since the way 'armies' and 'terrorists' or 'war' and 'terrorism' function is quite the opposite. Waging a war on terror is misdirection of funds and resources for measly returns. A terrorist cell, unlike an army, does not deploy 30,000 troops to fight its enemies. It needs only a handful of men, or women, to do a specific terror job in a soft location. Al-Qaeda had a representative government in Taliban to run Afghanistan hence it was quite easy to uproot the 'visible' Taliban but not the 'elusive' Al-Qaeda and its loyalists who still are the missing pieces. When everyday human activities become increasingly influenced by global forces terrorism is no exception. It is no

32.Gabriel Weimann, *Terrorists and Their Tools—Part II*, Yale Global, 26th April 2004, http://yaleglobal.yale.edu
33.ibid
34.BBC, *Tackling terror with technology*, 21st September, 2001, http://news.bbc.co.uk

longer local. It, too, has become global. The 9/11 terrorist attack, (for instance), was "… conceived in Afghanistan, nurtured in Germany, developed in Britain and financed through international banks."[35] Because terrorism operates through an invisible global network, it makes it even harder to confront it, let alone eliminate it, through war. The IRA (Irish Republican Army) has never been liquidated. The ETA (Euskadi Ta Askatasuna) is still alive in Spain. The Hamas are unyielding in Palestine. The LTTE is able to revive its attacks at any time. The numberless terror cells operating in Kashmir remain unrestrained. The Chechen rebels have not flattened out yet by the Russians.

Policies work more effectively than sending soldiers to fight shadow terrorists. The security situation in the U.S. has improved much more than what it was before 9/11. Thanks to improved domestic law enforcement, sharing of intelligence between countries, apprehension and extradition of terrorists, and tighter controls on terrorists' assets.[36] Pundits in Pentagon may claim that such effective policies have worked in minimizing the risk of threat to America but the heart of the argument is that such policies still could have been employed without having the need to chase invisible terrorists and create much more chaos in an already unruly Middle East and the rest of the world.

The limits of a terrorist's toolkit

If only all the previous terrorist attacks had changed the behaviour of world governments in favour of terrorists by budging to their fanaticism then one would claim a victory for terrorism. If there was any change in the behaviour of governments worldwide it only has become more strident in confronting the evil of terrorism by constricting the means terrorists would love to utilize to realize their ugly acts of murder and mayhem. Nor have regular terrorist attacks dented the spirit of commuters, holidaymakers, and businessmen who constantly defy the odds of a terrorist attack wherever they go. They still fly, sail, and commute. Terrorists are, in actuality, a lot weaker than they would like to portray themselves to popular imagination.

What is the maximum damage a terrorist can do, like the Twin Tower demolition? What would happen if terrorists managed to bring ideologically polarized countries, for instance, pitting Iran against America, to war? What if terrorists turned multi-ethnic, multi-religious or multi-cultural communities into battle-

---

35. Philippe Legrain, Philippe Legrain, *Open World*, (London, Abacus, 2002), p. 115
36. Audra K. Grant, The MIPT Terrorism Annual 2004

grounds such as turning Muslims against the Hindus, or vice versa, in India? These are rational questions planted with seeds of exaggeration often mushrooming fears in the minds of the public.

As much as they could, terrorists, in their ugly tradition, have always tried their best to create maximum damage to people and property, contrived to bring nations to war and bombed to incite civil mayhem and to divide societies by creating religious riots. Terrorists are ever laborious—scheming, plotting, and conspiring at their next act of mass carnage. Nevertheless, in the face of repeated terrorist attacks the world has grown to become more resilient. And, it energetically keeps trudging along.

As terrorism has increasingly come to be seen as part of everyday life a general consensus, though reluctantly accepted, that the world is not immune to terrorism is taking root in the public psyche. People around the world have come to accept the inevitability of having to live in the midst of terrorist threats and terrorists. When people accept something as part of their everyday lives the negativity of such a reality becomes diluted in its forcefulness. So is the case with terrorism. According to a poll in Germany, terrorism was not even seen to be in the top ten threats worrying the Germans as concerns about cuts in social benefits and loss of jobs seemed more pressing than a terrorist bomb. The possibility of a terrorist attack comes in only 14th, with 25 percent mentioning it—even fewer than those who are most concerned by global warming and climate change (38 percent).[37]

There was a period when Algeria creaked under the jaws of terrorism. It was also a period when religious terrorism put Algeria at the mercy of bloodiest barbarism of armed terror. Islamist terrorists in Algeria have caused the death of perhaps a quarter of a million people since 1992 and lasted until 1997. But today they are farther away from achieving power than ever. If anything, their brand of Islamism has lost all chances of ever finding a place in Algerian polity. Narrowly intent on unleashing 'Jihad in Algeria' the Armed Islamic Group (GIA) set off a series of terror attacks on unarmed civilians and security service. The group's activities ranged from bombing buildings, raping women, sabotage, mutilation of human bodies, and torture to deliberate criminal acts.

It was a kind of terrorism aimed at and determined to liquidate all strata of Algerian society. It was aimed to impose a theocratic state through massacre and destruction. What seemed an apparent strength of such terror tactics—killing and maiming and destroying—eventually turned out to be its inherent weakness. Fortunately, the involvement of the population in reaction against the atrocities,

---

37. *The Economist*, Terrorism in Germany, 26th August, 2005, p. 31

carried out on a huge scale by the terrorist groups, has forced them to retreat towards the mountains, where they are isolated from the population. They have begun to split up and their struggle has degenerated into acts of banditry and the settling of scores between rival factions.[38]

Terrorist wars in Turkey and Egypt in the 1980s and 1990s claimed more than 60,000 lives. But the terrorists won nothing, apart from the curse of the people and, perhaps, eternal damnation. Less than four years after 9/11 New York is more buoyant than ever, its property prices sky-rocketing while it hosts a record number of businesses and visitors ... (while) London ... was back to its normal life moments after the 7/7 suicide attacks.[39] One of the best examples of the failure of terrorism was when a series of bombs exploded in crowded trains in Mumbai in 2006. The attacks were carried out with the intention to bring India down to its knees, to disrupt the country's multi-faceted cultures, traditions, and more importantly the relations between Hindus and Muslims nurtured on strong democratic foundations, to cripple the city of Mumbai—the financial capital of India and to force India to give up its claim on Kashmir.

Unfortunately, for the terrorists, none of their aims bore fruit. International support for the government stood firm and sympathies for victims and their families profusely poured forth from various corners of the globe. Indians, regardless of their multiple identities, mainly Hindus and Muslims, refused to fall prey to tribal instincts, displaying exemplary solidarity. The Sensex, India's stock index, shot up by 3 points conveying a telling message to the terrorists that Mumbai's commercial spirit was hale and healthy. There was no instant knee-jerk reaction from India accusing Pakistan's leadership of its direct hand in the blasts. Without calling off the peace talks, India put a temporary brake on the peace process. For his part, Pakistan's President General Pervez Musharraf condemned the killing. The following morning, Mumbai was normal—and, back in business. While rail network was restored trains dutifully rattled along with unremitting commuters packed to their fill.[40]

38.M Boudjemaa, Monograph No. 74, *Terrorism in Algeria: Ten years of Day-to-Day Genocide, Africa and terrorism*, Joining the Global Campaign, Edited by Jakkie Cilliers and Kathryn Sturman, http://www.iss.co.za

39.Amir Taheri, *Terrorism Cannot Win: This Is Why*, Asharq Alawsat, 29th July, 2005, http://aawsat.com/english/news.asp?section=2&id=1011

40.Kavin Kanagasabai, Se7en Magazine, *Terror on the tracks*, Issue 63, August 18—September 01, 2006 http://www.se7enmagazine.org

Terrorists historically have failed to alter the shape of a society, let alone transform it to their wish. Terrorists, with all their insidious power to wreak havoc, have always failed to get the majority support. They are limited by their resources, both intellectual and physical, unless rogue States collude with them to supply chemical, biological or nuclear material and let them loose with their blessings. Employing hi-tech weapons is surely not as easy as pressing the trigger of a detonator nor is it as less challenging as packing a human with a bomb. It is complex and therefore, a time-consuming exercise. Chemical agents are easy to acquire or produce but difficult to keep them in stable condition and their functioning largely depends on climatic conditions. Biological agents are more potent and lethal. If chemical agents could kill only thousands, biological weapons could extend its victims to hundreds of thousands. They may not be difficult to procure but could be very tricky to store and disperse. Its deadly nature means that the risk of contamination of those handling such agents is very high and, most of the lethal bacteria and spores do not survive well outside the laboratory. That rules out the practical effectiveness of using biological weapons. The inherent technical difficulties with these weapons make handling of biological and nuclear materials hard for terrorists wanting to use them.

Terrorists are not only limited in their support from the general public, they are restricted in their access to using weapons of mass destruction too. The fact that terrorists so far have not used nuclear material is because of the technicalities involved in their production, manufacture, storage, and delivery. More importantly, executing such a complexity-driven operation has the difficulty of bypassing the eagle-eyed attention of international vigilante and non-stop scrutiny. Not just in weaponry are terrorists disadvantaged but also intellectually, as they are also intellectually bankrupt in seeing the wider differences of mankind.

A terrorist resorts to cold-blooded murder because of his inability to engage in debate or discussion or dialogue to resolve conflicts arising in human engagement in a civilized way. The recourse to 'killing' people is actually an inherent weakness in a terrorist's arsenal. It is not just Islamist terrorists but also terrorists of different shades who are basically products of hardened 'ideologies' who are utterly incapable of engaging themselves in active politics since it requires developing policies which they are utterly incapable of; of bringing about social development as it requires promotion of social harmony, of tolerance and of secular values in a globalizing world; and of creating viable economic conditions for it demands the establishment of basic needs for people such as building roads, hospitals, schools and so on. Reacting against Salman Rushdie's novel by decreeing for his death is a less painful exercise than challenging him intellectually through debate and logic. Stabbing Theo Van Gogh, the Dutch film maker who made a controversial film, Submission, on Islam, was less burdensome than producing an alternative documentary countering his points of view constructively. Catering to the basic needs of people, writing a book or making a film requires not just time but also intellectually painstaking hard work. Planting a bomb in a car does not.

Relying on the tools of terrorism to spread the 'glory' of Islam will hardly win supporters to the cause of Islam. Terrorists do not come out in the open to confront real issues affecting both the individual and the society. They work within secret cells and perform guerrilla war. Islamists, in their fervent endeavour to spread their message of anger and frustration, consciously or unconsciously end up destroying their own peoples' welfare, their livelihood and ultimately the very image of their religion. Even where terrorists attract admiration, they end up by wrecking the home base. The more attacks they launch, the greater the harm to other Muslims, either because terrorist attacks are deliberately indiscriminate; or because, as in Luxor, Marrakesh, and Indonesia, their targets are not only tourist infidels but the "corrupting" tourism industry upon which millions of livelihoods depend. There is no *modus vivendi* with groups that define all those who question their obscurantist distortions of Islam as "enemies of the Faith" and consider compromise a mortal sin, so societies have to choose. Once these cancer cells have become established, it may take long and terrible civil wars, as it did in Algeria and may in Palestine and, yet again, in Afghanistan, to wither them. But Islamist terrorists cannot ultimately rely on acquiring critical mass, the secret of all successful revolutions.[41]

Terrorism contains within itself its own seeds of destruction. However, to remain complacent is to depreciate the dangers that terrorism poses to communal peace and to undermine the task of keeping the threat under control. Terrorists will keep hitting so long as they choose physical violence and destruction as means of expression to convey their frustration and anger causing damage, carnage and extermination. Doubtless, in the long run they surely will be dead.

---

41. *The Times*, Why the Islamists will never win, August 12, 2006

CHAPTER 4

▼

THE PERTINENCE OF HUMAN RIGHTS

Human beings live in a society. If each one of us were to live a solitary life in an island then this very subject would be supererogatory. Because we have no choice other than to live together, we need a harmonious orchestration of existence so as to make our 'life' and 'living' peaceful and blithesome. It is a nauseating spectacle to see one man's violation of another man's rights looming ahead—macabre acts of exploitation, torture, and murder are perpetrated against fellow human beings in the name of religion, in the name of politics, in the name of justice and what not.

Crimes against men, women, and children are so commonplace in politically authoritarian, brutal, exploitative societies that they hardly smite the conscience of their leaders, and have only severed the entity of civility as surely as a surgeon's scalpel severs the bone and flesh of a limb in an amputation. The bitter reality we see today right from Cuba to Cameroon to China is that in unmitigated insouciance to human rights, their leadership, or the lack of it, has mastered to hew man's rights.

Absence of fundamental rights for peoples in dictatorial and authoritarian countries has left the face of humanity shorn. In places like Iraq respect for human dignity has fallen in the puddles of gore; or it is licking the wounds of ethnic violence in Sudan; or humiliated to the hilt in Guantanamo Bay. Of all the powerful nuclear weapons in the world, of all the savage beasts in the jungle, of all the poisonous plants in the forest, man stands as the most dangerous threat to another man's life. For he often gets caught off guard, sometimes injuriously and sometimes fatally, by the system he is stuck in. "Rights, in fact, are those conditions of social life without which no man can seek, in general, to be himself at his best". These words of Harold J. Laski cogently delineate that to live a wholesome life with dignity and respect, man has to be bestowed with basic rights he deserves. Rights, doubtless, are the economic, political and social privileges to which one has just, moral and legal claim.

The concept of human rights dates back to 6th century BC during the reign of Cyrus the Great when the Persian Empire established the principles of Human Rights. Three centuries later the Mauryan Empire of Ashoka the Great, in ancient India, mandated the unprecedented principles of civil rights in the 3rd century BC. The Magna Carta, also known as the Great Charter, issued by King John after he was forced to sign it defined the limits of the feudal rights of the King, thereby requiring the King to renounce certain rights, respect certain legalities and recognize that the will of the King was bound by law. It was a historical landmark in the annals of human rights that clearly put confines over what an individual with political power could and could not do. The 18th century was witness to major revolutions—in the United States it led to the country's declaration of independence from Britain spurred by the belief that "all men are created equal, that they are endowed by their creator with certain unalienable rights that among these are life, liberty and the pursuit of happiness." In France, the thirst for human rights culminated in its 1789 revolution which made the slogan "Liberté, Égalité, Fraternité" universally popular while scores of philosophers such as John Locke, Thomas Paine, and John Stuart Mill attached utmost importance to the 'rights of man'. In 1917 the Russian Revolution highlighted the struggle for human rights that brought about the demise of autocracy in Russia. In the 20th century the International Labour Organisation recognized the human rights through adherence to workers' rights, their working conditions, training, health and safety.

Human Rights, today, has become a burning issue acquiring the central focus in the compass of global vision. The Charter of the United Nations staunchly emphasizes in its Article 55 that the World body "shall promote universal respect for, and observance of, human rights and fundamental freedom for all without distinction as to race, sex, language, or religion", and ensures its commitment in the ensuing Article 56 that the member States "pledge themselves to take joint and separate action in cooperation with the Organization for the achievement of the purposes set forth in Article 55".

Deplorably, several member States of the United Nations are themselves party to the brazenness exhibited in the violation of human rights. The overt abuse of rights of man has fusilladed the constitutional laws and humanism into insignificance as it kicked the bottom out of the moral legitimacy that any dispensation could claim and culminated in the trampling upon of all established canons of human propriety. The grave threat to personal life, liberty and protection disconcertingly sweeps across in authoritarian societies where human lives are abused, uncared and unvalued. In spite of increasing global prosperity and a yearning among people for more freedom, the itch to restrict human freedom has not disappeared altogether. Many parts of the world are still stricken by the contagion of its virus.

Even the so-called civilized countries such as the United States and Britain have become party to gross human rights abuse. United States has a long standing record of its abuse of prisoners in Guantanamo Bay on top of its soldiers' involvement in the sexual abuse of prisoners in Abu Ghraib prison in Iraq. Such crass debasement of human rights speaks volumes of harrowing extravagance several innocent men had to undergo the blatant cruelty at the quirks and twists of those into whose hands power has been invested. The involvement of American and British soldiers in the abuse of ordinary Iraqis in their idealistic quest for bringing democracy in Iraq is an indication of how, in the name of peace-keeping, the lives of ordinary men, women and children are shredded into pieces. North Korea, notorious for secrecy, has a dubious reputation for its abysmally loutish human rights record. It stands as one of the world's most repressive regimes. It is not alone. It has some others—the likes of Zimbabwe, Burma, Tanzania, Iran, China, and Cuba—in company who excel in the art of suppression of their innocent citizens.

Despite sturdy international recognition of laws to protect and respect man's life, what we witness everyday in repressive regimes is a litany of ghastly acts of human rights violations grazing into the vitals of human lives. The denial of justice or the delay of redress or the disdain of sensitivity to uphold human values only foments volumes of the scalding magma of gangrene from which 'the rights of man' is fast perishing.

The masters of yesteryear human slavery—Britain and the United States, abolished slavery in 1833 and 1862 respectively. Sadly, human slavery has not disappeared completely. The Anti-Slavery International, founded in 1839, is the oldest human rights organisation. The fact that it is still in business is an indication of slavery being practiced in several countries across the globe. Well and truly, slavery is very much in business.

According to the Anti-Slavery International, slavery continues to this day with a modern face—bonded labour, early and forced marriage, forced labour, slavery by descent (slave labour involving people who are seen as belonging to a slave class or are from a group deemed fit for slave job), trafficking and worst forms of child labour. In Sudan, women and children are abducted and sold to government-backed militias. In Brazil, peasants clear the jungle at gunpoint. In Ghana, small girls are offered as sexual playthings to village priests by way of reparation for "transgressions" committed by other family members, living or dead. In Western Europe and the United States, east Europeans, Chinese, Vietnamese and other immigrants work against their will in prostitution, domestic service, farms and sweatshops.[1] In Britain, where human rights abuse is taken seriously, the booming sex trade where young women are forced into the industry ruthlessly remained largely untouched for some time. According to a report in The Daily Telegraph, "an "alarming" number of young women, mostly east Europeans aged 18 to 25, (were) held captive in privately owned flats and houses and forced to have sex with up to 30 "clients" a day."[2]

It would be quite premature and very wrong to assume that civilization has made the peoples of the world decent and humane. The truth is quite the contrary. A report by the International Labour Organisation suggests a minimum of 12.3 million (slaves in the world today). Others say the figure is closer to 27 million. The majority are in Asia and Latin America[3] where democracy and the rule of law are either flawed or partially or fully absent. (Yet), politically, some progress has been made in recent years, with new UN and EU conventions against trafficking, and new policies against bonded labour in Asia. But although countries may sign up to international agreements and express their opposition to slavery, prosecutions are rare.[4] In several countries, opposition to slavery, enactment of anti-slavery legislation, and implementation of anti-slavery law still remain nothing more than mere cosmetic gesture.

---

1. *The Economist—The World in 2007*, Of inhuman bondage, 21st Edition, (Annual Publication) p. 100
2. *The Sunday Telegraph*, Sex trade moves its modern-day slaves into the suburbs, 18th February, 2007
3. *The Economist—The World in 2007*, Of inhuman bondage
4. ibid

Many forms of discrimination—gender, race, colour of skin, ethnicity, caste, religion, nationality and the like—today have become illegal. With too many events taking place every fraction of a second around the globe it is hard to measure whether repression worldwide is going down or shooting upwards. But surely and certainly, awareness of human rights abuse has increased manifold with the help of media and organisations such as Amnesty International, Human Rights Watch, Freedom House, and countless other organisations who work and promote the tenets of human values and bring out any form of human abuse to the attention of the outside world.

People have always valued their freedom and liberty and rights but more and more people today have come to realize the importance of their rights as individuals and what those rights would mean for their freedom and liberty. In this aspect, globalization has brought boon to many bane lives around the world. Silence often feeds oppression. That oppression now is voiced against by the growing solidarity among peoples of the world who believe in individual freedom and liberty. Globalization and global integration, in this regard, brought voice to the voiceless many. The world, today, is more aware and more alert to human rights abuses.

Ever since Slobodan Milosevic, Serbia's president, became the first head of state since the Second World War, to be charged with and arrested for war crimes there have been others who are now waiting to face the law. Charles Taylor, Liberia's president, charged with war crimes and crimes against humanity in 2003, is to be tried by the Special Court for Sierra Leone. Saddam Hussein, the Iraqi dictator, was executed after being convicted of war crimes by a special court in Iraq even though the process of justice was considered highly partisan and heavily flawed. The fact that Saddam was meted out a death sentence was largely and mainly due to his crimes against humanity. Recently, Mengistu Haile Mariam, a communist and ex-president of Ethiopia was convicted of genocide in absentia for his role in a domestic terrorism campaign known as the Red Terror.

There are other political leaders too around the world who are being put under trial. Juan María Bordaberry, the former Uruguayan dictator, was arrested in 2006 for the murder of opposition leaders in 1976 during his dictatorship. In the meanwhile, leaders such as Alberto Fujimori for his role in human rights abuses and corruption in Peru and Luis Echeverría, former president of Mexico, for the massacre of student protesters are waiting to be in the dock for their brutalities on people. Augusto Pinochet's old-age, senility and death helped him avoid facing the trials for his atrocities on human rights when he was the president of Chile but his arrest in London in 1998, indeed, served as a precursor to the future trials of political tyrants in the new millennium.

For the first time in the history of the world, no world leader can cosily sit in power ordering or ignoring the crass as well as gross abuse of his people with utter impunity. Nevertheless, the amount of awareness the world is exposed to crimes against humanity is a sure sign of progress in the curtailment, if not the eradication, of human abuse. Despite efforts to eliminate human rights violations globally, it is still a world of human crimes coloured by brutality, violence and disrespect dotting the human landscape with its stain of viciousness.

Not in my backyard

The aftermath of removal of Taliban in Afghanistan as a result of the 'war on terror' launched after the terrorist attack on America on September 11, 2001 saw a wave of prisoners, branded as 'enemy combatants' who were seized during the war in Afghanistan suspected to be aiding al-Qaeda or fighting for Taliban, imprisoned in Guantanamo Bay in Cuba. Hundreds of individuals from a mishmash of nationalities were detained indefinitely as they remain trapped in a legal quagmire that appears to be unending. The individuals are denied access to court, legal redress and family visits. Guantanamo Bay now stands as a symbol of American cruelty, injustice, and double-standards making America's commitment to democratic norms look virtuous on paper but vile in practice. The fact that America is sincere, relatively, to its human rights protection within its boundaries but does exactly the opposite outside of them betrays the double-standards of its talk of democracy and human rights.

The impression America dishes out to the rest of the world by denying basic rights to the 'prisoners' is unworthy of a nation that had long cherished and saw itself as a beacon of human rights, liberty and freedom. The values that made America what is today are crushed under an ill-thought out plan of 'war on terror' which has already nosedived into an embarrassing failure. Apart from creating a verbal spin on the logic of 'war on terror' it remains as effective as any other sloganeering stunt—such as the war on drugs, war on poverty, war on AIDS which nevertheless refuse to die out—we frequently hear day in and day out that keeps fighting without an end in sight and without stemming the source.

Besides alienating many governments through its hegemonic adherence to 'war on terror', America stands itself amidst the throes of international suspicion. Worse still, its brushing aside of Geneva Conventions which calls for an independent tribunal to hear the prisoners' status quo, has not helped either. The U.S. has claimed that all persons captured in the "global war on terror" are "enemy combatants" who may be detained without charges for the duration of the conflict.[5] That the hostages are not ordinary prisoners of war, nor are they usual criminals to be dealt with in accordance with international law does not justify the inhuman treatment that they are subjected to. The hostages are not from al-Qaeda wing alone to be labelled as "enemy combatants." In fact, there are others who fought for the Taliban government, and therefore qualify as 'prisoners of war' in every legal sense.

Precious times of lives are lost by delaying justice to the prisoners. It is inhuman to confine people indefinitely into dark cells of pain, alienation from families, and uncertainty of their future. Justice delayed is justice denied. It is also a denial of democratic rights. To deny justice under one pretext or another is to shut all means to the door of justice. If no evidence is found to incriminate the prisoners, it is villainous prejudice to keep the prisoners chained for the duration of the 'war on terror' which no one knows when, where and how will end. One is either guilty or not guilty. To let people tread between the hazy line of guilt and innocence with an uncertain future bespeaks of human insensitivity, political irresponsibility and legal profanity.

As if America's abuses at Guantanamo Bay were not enough, its invasion of Iraq fetched some more prisoners who were piled into the Abu Ghraib prison. The Iraqi prisoners too were not exempt from abuses. The Iraqi prisoners were treated differently in comparison to their counterparts in Guantanamo Bay in the sense that they were defiled in their person through the "... guard dogs snarling at cowering prisoners (to) Iraqi women being forced to expose their breasts ..."[6] to other forms of humiliation and torture. Apart from the American hand, British contribution to abuse added an additional dash of tribulation to the plight of Iraqi prisoners.

The episode of despicable treatment of Iraqi prisoners, sexually and physically, and psychologically, both by American and British soldiers throwing all norms of decorum and decency to the wind is just another instance of utter disregard for human rights dumped into the dirty heap of extremely crude incivility. It is one thing to seek sanctuary behind an excuse that only a few bad soldiers, sometimes, besmirch an otherwise 'noble' operation, out of frustration and irrationality, intended to bring freedom to a suppressed people. It is quite another to keep pro-

---

5. Human Rights Watch, Questions and Answers, *U.S. Detainees Disappeared into Secret Prisons: Illegal under Domestic and International Law, December 9, 2005*.http://hrw.org

6. *The Guardian*, 1,800 new pictures add to US disgust, 13th May, 2004

longing an environment conducive to breeding similar abuses by delaying justice. The idea of bringing freedom to those parts of the world where the rule of tyranny prevails cannot be achieved through force, and it surely must not be through abuse. Doing so spoils the very ideal of human dignity, freedom and respect which civilized societies seek to uphold.

Political capital at the cost of freedom

In the developing world many authoritarian regimes which are also economically vibrant often tend to entertain the notion that 'economic growth' is possible only when individual freedom is abbreviated. Such a notion springs out of the argument that it is better for an individual to be in political chains than to be in economic chains.

Absolute poverty has fallen in China ever since the opening of its economy to the world. The gloss with which modern China is marching towards economic global stardom has veiled the plight of several millions of its citizens subjected to excessive political containment. There are "… farmers being beaten to death for complaining about embezzlement, officials conniving to hoodwink Communist Party leaders about production levels, and a tax system which forces the poor in effect to subsidize the rich minority. It helps to explain the exodus of workers from farms to low-paid, often dangerous jobs in the booming coastal provinces or Europe and America."[7]

Whatever stories escape out of the tightly capped media, of the political atrocities unleashed on ordinary Chinese including the rulers' intolerance of dissent, of the regime's paranoia of popular uprising, of the poverty of laws to granting basic freedoms for people to question government policies, of the free-hand to torture and mistreat prisoners, of forced confessions, of indefinite as well as of incommunicado detention, of harsh prison conditions, they form only the tiny tip of the iceberg. A large part of politically blessed abuse is buried underneath the calm oasis of a country that is floating on a wave of new-found wealth. Restrictions on freedom of speech, curbs on media freedom, and restraints on the right to form assemblies or disallowing the practice of religion, forge the backbone of a centrally-controlled authoritarian rule in China.

Often, the disaffection among the communist-prone leaders to attach any importance to political freedom arises from the failure to distinguish between 'human rights' and 'human needs'. The ambiguity between "needs" and "rights"

---

7. *The Telegraph*, Exposé of poverty in China shames regime, 25th February, 2004

as to their relevance and importance requires clarity. The liberty to 'question' the policies or programmes of the State, if and when they are deemed ineffective, is different from the basic needs which are to be satisfied by the State. Various resolutions and declarations of the United Nations list—as human rights—benefits like full employment, vacations with pay, maternity leave, and free medical care.[8] Indiscriminate inclusion of such basic fulfilment of rights often supports the claims of leftist ideologues that even totalitarian States respect human rights. An individual's right to claim basic necessities of life are not the same as the right to demand answers from an erring government.

Besides, the leftist ideologues "… contend that while free democracies have a better record in certain areas of human rights, authoritarian States have a superior record in other areas. It was such depreciation of the currency of human rights which emboldened Lenin to proclaim that the Soviets represent a "higher form of democracy" and Hitler to claim to be an "arch democrat"; and which enables States that practice torture and ruthless repression at home to pay pious lip service to human rights at international forums.[9]

The leftist argument against the irrelevance of human rights in the realm of polity is only relative. The importance of individual freedom and rights may be missed when things go well and everything is routinely predictable.

Authoritarian regimes may sometimes take a country to prosperity but only to slide it backwards eventually. Indonesia under Suharto is an apt example. Suharto may have improved the economic well-being of some of Indonesia's citizens for a time, but his cronyism, corruption, and autocratic governance ultimately caused the collapse of both his own regime and the Indonesian economy. By contrast, President Kim Dae Jung of South Korea was able to help his country weather its economic storm in the late 1990s (during the Asian financial crisis) by enacting austerity measures that a majority of citizens deemed legitimate because of Kim's democratic mandate.[10]

Another form of human rights abuse is the politically influenced death penalty with the involvement of a twisted criminal justice system for non-violent crimes. When an individual is executed for non-violent crimes such tax evasion or embezzlement, it is the epitome of cancer afflicting both judiciary and polity. In China,

---

8. Nani A. Palkhivala, *We, The Nation*, (New Delhi, UBS, 1994), p. 24
9. ibid, p. 25
10. John Shattuck, Diplomacy with a cause: Human Rights in U.S. foreign policy, *Realizing Human Rights*, Edited by Samantha Power, Graham Allison, Chapter Twelve, p 275

claims Amnesty International (AI) in its 2005 Report, the death penalty for civil crimes such as tax fraud and embezzlement as well as drug offences and violent crimes is carried out extensively and arbitrarily, at times as a result of political interference. AI further reports that an estimated 3,400 people had been executed and at least 6,000 sentenced to death, although the true figures were believed to be much higher. In March (2004), a senior member of the National People's Congress announced that China executes around 10,000 people per year. A lack of basic safeguards protecting the rights of defendants meant that large numbers of people continued to be sentenced to death and executed after unfair trials.[11]

It is not just China that leads in the abuse of human rights. There are other countries such as North Korea and Cuba that share the same values of ill-treating their own citizens. What makes it worse is with the media muffled and muzzled, much of the abuse taking place within their geographical confines remains away from the purview of the world.

Already reeling under widespread chronic malnutrition, both children and urban adults in the Northern Province in North Korea are subject to further food crisis. On top of government crackdown on fundamental rights, freedom of expression as well as association and movement, executions by firing squad or hanging, molestation of women detainees in degrading prison conditions and torture and ill-treatment, millions of North Koreans are in dire need of food as the government controls all political, economic and social activities from the centre, and with an iron fist. Rations from the Public Distribution System—the primary source of staple food for more than 70 percent of the population were reportedly set to decline from the already insufficient 310g per person in 2003 to 300g in 2004.[12]

The North Korean penal code is such that theft of food is punishable by death! Any work or activity related to press or religion comes under the scrutiny of stringent government eye. The trade unions are controlled by State, hence the State is supreme. A genuine problem identified by a trade union may still be discarded as insignificant by the State. The elite class in the country are provided with modern medicine and facilities while the rest of the population cannot even go near the basic supplies such as bandages or antibiotics. For those who habitually demonize capitalism must look at the plight of North Korean workers withering under socialist ideology and their trade unions, while the believers in the virtues of authoritarianism need only look at the state of the North Korea's

---

11. Amnesty International, *Report 2005*, China
12. ibid, North Korea

healthcare. On the one hand, North Korea's economic socialism is preventing the people from having right of access to meet their basic needs, while on the other hand its political authoritarianism is stifling their freedom and independence.

Cuba, over the last few years, has designed an effective tool of repression: its constitution. The license to deny civil and political freedom is diligently carved in its laws. In the name of law, the state comes down heavily even on silent dissent with a weighty prison sentence, threats of prosecution and even exile. Fundamental rights such as assembly, association and expression are grossly intolerated. Cuba ranks as the only country in the Western Hemisphere to have shunned political pluralism, democracy, and freedom, as the country's government is greatly inclined toward tightening its totalitarian leash on its citizens and negating them any sort of political, economic or human rights.

Cubans have neither the privilege nor the pleasure to change their governments through democratic means. Cuba's dictatorial leader, Fidel Castro, confiscated power by knocking over his predecessor, the US-backed dictator, Fulgencio Batista in the year 1959. Since that day to the present, Castro dictates the life and liberty of Cubans unreservedly. As the only self-proclaimed voice of Cuba's citizens, Castro is responsible for the appointment of Council of Ministers. He rules the country not just as Head of State and Chief of Government. He is also the Chairman of the Council of State, Commander-in-Chief of the Revolutionary Armed Forces, President of the Council of Ministers and first Secretary of the Communist Party of Cuba. It is as if hell had given all its powers into his hands.

Political imprisonment in the country still continues as an ugly everyday-reality. In 2005, "... the Cuban Commission for Human Rights and National Reconciliation ... issued a list of 306 prisoners who it said were incarcerated for political reasons.... Of seventy-five political dissidents, independent journalists, and human rights advocates who were summarily tried in April 2003, sixty-one remained imprisoned. Serving sentences that average nearly twenty years, the incarcerated dissidents endure poor conditions and punitive treatment in prison."[13] Even though severe health problems affected several prisoners, it failed to evoke the responsive chord of a callous dictatorial administration for a humanitarian release from prison.

Ordinary Cubans do not even have the elementary liberty to travel freely. Official permission has to be sought prior to travel, which according to the Human Rights Watch, is often denied. Criminal prosecution follows anyone daring to travel outside or returning to Cuba without official permission. The

---

13.Human Rights Watch, *World Report 2006*, Cuba, pp187–188

regime even goes to the extent of taking children hostage so as to ensure the return of their parents when they travel overseas.

Torture still remains a tool of repression of countries devoted to totalitarian ideals. Governments' careless and frequent recourse to acts of cruel, inhuman, or degrading treatment of their dissenting citizens to extract confessions so that they are forced to admitting to spying or conspiracy activities against national interests are all too common. A China or a North Korea or a Cuba is no stranger to the medieval practice of this barbaric act. What is more surprising is that the United States, often the moralizer to countries with dubious records on human rights, is itself no stranger to torture. America's detainees in prison are spread over from Afghanistan to Iraq to Guantanamo Bay as well as in its secret detention centres. At least 26 prisoners are said to have died in American custody in Iraq and Afghanistan since 2002 in what Army and Navy investigators have concluded or suspected were acts of criminal homicide.[14]

As one of the founding members of United Nations, United States blatantly flouts the UN Convention against Torture which defines torture as "any act by which severe pain or suffering, whether physical or mental, is intentionally inflicted on a person for such purposes as obtaining from him or a third person information or a confession, punishing him for an act he or a third person has committed or is suspected of having committed, or intimidating or coercing him or a third person, or for any reason based on discrimination of any kind, when such pain or suffering is inflicted by or at the instigation of or with the consent or acquiescence of a public official or other person acting in an official capacity."[15]

Poverty is a double-edged sword. It can both be a cause and a product of human rights abuse. The link between the two is obvious. People whose rights are denied—victims of discrimination or persecution, for example—are more likely to be poor. Generally they find it harder or impossible to participate in the labour market and have little or no access to basic services and resources. Meanwhile, the poor in many societies cannot enjoy their rights to education, health and housing simply because they cannot afford them. And poverty affects all human rights: for example, low income can prevent people from accessing education—an "economic and social" right—which in turn inhibits their participation

---

14. *The New York Times*, The Conflict in Iraq: Detainees; U.S. Military Says 26
    Inmate Deaths May Be Homicide, 16th March, 2005, Section A, Page 1
15. Office of the High Commissioner for Human Rights, Convention Against
    Torture and Other Cruel, Inhuman or Degrading Treatment or
    Punishment, Part 1, Article 1

in public life—a "civil and political" right—and their ability to influence policies affecting them.[16] As people become powerless, incapacitated, and vulnerable they become mere puppets in the hands of their rulers.

It may not be wrong to say that poor states are also the most authoritarian ones or socially rived or politically and socially unstable. Take the case of Sudan. It is the largest African country by area. It is one of the poorest countries in the world where the "poverty rate in the south is 90 percent (50 percent in north)"[17] and ranked at 141st place out of 177 countries in the Human Development Index (2006), conducted by the United Nations Development Programme. Sudan was once part of the Kush kingdom from the 8th century BC to 350 AD and later came under the influence of Christianity in the 6th century. Between the 13th and 15th centuries, it fell under Muslim control, thus Islam became Sudan's principal religion. The north remained predominantly Muslim while the south comprised practitioners of either Christianity or traditional beliefs. The Muslim north has always been richer than the poor non-Muslim south.

The relation between the north and the south is often marked with tension, unrest and revolt. Before its independence in 1956, a civil war broke out between the north and the south. The smouldering discontent between the Arabic north and the Christian and animist south erupted once again. It lasted for 17 years from 1955 to 1972. The war was to happen again—this time in 1982 when the introduction of Islamic (Sharia) Law sparked fresh bouts of unrest. The year 1989 brought Omar Hassan Ahmed al-Bashir, a military General, to power to become the President and chief of state, Prime Minister and chief of the armed forces. It was the convergence of all absolute power absolutely into one man's hands. Since the day that brought him into power, he, to this day, remains the undisputed leader of Sudan.

The conflict that surfaced, yet again, in 2003, in the western region of Darfur resulted in tens of thousands of deaths and millions displaced. Many of Darfur's 6 (million) inhabitants have been raped and massacred by militias armed by their own government. Some 300,000 people have died in the conflict; over 2 (million) have been herded into camps.[18]

---

16. National Human Rights Institutions Forum, *Human Rights Day*, 10th December, 2006, www.nhri.net

17. Reuters Alert Net, FACTBOX—*Sudan, one of the world's poorest countries*, 12th April, 2005, www.alertnet.org

18. *The Economist*, Never say never again, February 23, 2006, http://www.economist.com

Amidst the killings in Darfur, China, a 'friend' of Sudan, loves the country's oil and other resources more than it cares for the lives of innocent civilians. China's oil purchases fill Sudan's coffers, part of which customarily gets channelled towards terror activities. China has invested about $15 billion in Sudan's oil projects; 7 percent of its oil-imports flow from Sudan or conversely Sudan pours 60 percent of its oil into China. It is a political marriage of convenience between a dictatorial communist regime, and a despotic Islamic government that shows compunction neither for human rights nor human lives. Amnesty International accused China of selling an array of weapons to human rights abusers such as Sudan and Myanmar. It is no surprise then that Chinese-made AK-47 rifles made their way to Darfur, and their bullets into the hearts of hundreds of thousands of victims. China staunchly stands by its friend Sudan despite the latter's continuing odious dalliance with genocide, or mass murder.[19]

Amnesty International lists out a litany of atrocities perpetrated under the aegis of Sudan government—ranging from unlawful extra-judicial killings carried out both by government forces and militias, violence on women including rape and sexual slavery, torture of detainees by security forces, police and military intelligence, deaths in custody, incommunicado detention, harassment and arrest of human rights workers, restrictions on freedom of expression and death penalty and other cruel, inhuman and degrading punishments. The discontent among the people, particularly those in the south, is an interconnection of historical frustration at corrupt rule at the centre and the failure to share the power and wealth with the impoverished peripheries of the country. That is in total contradiction, both in spirit and in practice, to the country's constitution which avows that "The State of Sudan is an embracing homeland, wherein races and cultures coalesce and religions conciliate.[20] Until the economic demands are met, until the alienated sections of Sudan are involved in the mainstream socio-political life, abuse of human rights will not entirely disappear. Widespread prosperity too will remain elusive.

The primary duty of any government is to protect life, dignity, and the rights of people that come under its jurisdiction and to uphold laws in the true spirit of

---

19. Kavin Kanagasabai, *Se7en Magazine*, The Darfur disintegration, Issue 63, July 22—August 4, 2006, http://www.se7enmagazine.org
20. The Constitution of The Republic of Sudan 1998, Part 1, The State and The Directive Principles, Nature of the State, The System of Government, www.sudan.gov.sd

respect for human rights. Contrary to being custodians of law and justice, villainous governments, in their madness for irrational self-interests, have shoved the laws under the rubble of torture, pain and death.

If poverty is about power, then solutions must focus on the empowerment of people themselves, especially those suffering the greatest discrimination and social exclusion. History is littered with well-meaning but failed 'top-down' solutions that overlook the root causes of poverty as well as the demands, perspectives, and capacities, of people themselves to be architects of their own destiny. Sustainable solutions will often depend on multi-faceted responses, aiming at a just redistribution of power relations, rather than quick fixes or one-off handouts.[21]

The politicization of judiciary

The entry of political interests into the portals of judiciary, which in the past may themselves have bended the laws in their favour to consume their political fruits, has forged a new culture—politicization of judiciary. To put it otherwise, it is the legalization of political crimes through alteration of laws. In democratic societies, such alteration has to go through the executive and must escape the brunt of a prying, sometimes hostile media and the cacophony of public debate. In totalitarian regimes or in authoritarian societies, outside intervention is conveniently prevented and muffled. In their schizophrenic scrambling for power, the Robert Mugabes, the Kim Jong Ils and the Saddam Husseins substituted the 'rule of law' with *their* 'rules of despotism'. Such flexing of rules transformed their countries into mob-led or crime-infested or hazard-filled societies.

Judiciary is the last citadel that can safeguard and restore the 'lost' rights of an individual, thereby dispensing justice. It is the soul of man's rights. When values, virtues and probity erode judiciary through its politicization it leads to abuse of law resulting in the betrayal and robbing of rights of individuals. Abuse of judiciary by vested-interests or exploitation of law by political interests can lead to, for example, a national disenchantment as in China, a proprietary paradise in Zimbabwe, or a proletariat limbo in North Korea. Politicization of judiciary is a tether in the hands of the politically powerful to chain and rule the politically-weak.

---

21. National Human Rights Institutions Forum, *Human Rights Day*,
www.nhri.net

Two and a half decades after the 'Islamic Revolution' the human rights situation in Iran remains pathetic. Apart from the restriction of the rights of its citizens, systematic abuses such as extra-judicial killings and summary executions, widespread use of torture, arbitrary arrest and detention without due legal process, unfair trials and suppression of religious minorities are perpetrated by the conservative elements of both the judiciary and security establishment.

Amnesty International, in a press release, highlighted the efforts by Iran's judiciary in curbing freedom of expression and association by encroaching on human rights and civil society activists. The judiciary has placed Iran's growing civil society under attack. The targeted arbitrary arrests and detention in secret places along with reports of ill treatment of activists and journalist(s) clearly expose the judiciary's intention to clamp down on Iran's burgeoning civil society.[22]

Political prisoners, prisoners of conscience, and people expressing their opinions through media are not spared from being promptly locked up inside the walled confines of Iranian jails. Scores of them are imprisoned, usually unfairly, on the pretext of being a 'national threat'. Notoriously tainted for its abuse of human liberty, courts in Iran express a willing assault on its subjects. The courts even conduct cases unconstitutionally to try political cases behind closed doors and 'rightfully' deny defendants any sort of access to their lawyers. That potentially renders the defendants weak to argue their case or to gather evidence to support their claim. Having said that, even providing with a lawyer or access to evidence to certain defendants will avail no benefit since people are imprisoned on charges as transcendental as 'enmity against God' or as non-violent as 'morality crimes' for which it is impossible or near to impossible to fetch evidence.

In its Report 2006, Amnesty International uncovers the fact that at least 94 people were executed in 2004, including at least eight people who were at least under 18 years of age at the time of their alleged offence. Many sentences of flogging were imposed. The true number of those executed or subjected to corporal punishment was believed to be considerably higher than the cases reported.[23] Laws and practices openly discriminating Iranians, especially those belonging to different religious and ethnic groups, have always been a source of political unrest and of human rights violations. Under 'gozinesh' or selection provisions, people are denied state employment due to their religious affiliation and political opinions as Iranian legal system assaults its people discriminatingly and selectively.

---

22. Amnesty International, *Iran: Civil society activists and human rights defenders under attack*, 10th November, 2004, http://www.amnesty.org

23. Amnesty International, *Report 2006*, Iran

The AI Report further points out the political stalemate that continued in its 2005 presidential election in which more than 1,000 presidential candidates were excluded from the election by the Council of Guardians, which reviews laws and policies for upholding Islamic tenets and the Constitution. What stood out in striking glare was the fact that all 89 women candidates were excluded on the basis of their 'gender' under Iran's discriminatory selection procedures.

When political leaders assume the responsibility of running the legal system in a country it creates a vacuum in the judiciary. Such political control of law grazes into the vitals of the judiciary. It renders the justice system ineffective, non-functional and into a mere rubber-stamp. When political interests drive the judicial process, legal machinery becomes a mute spectator. An independent judiciary requires both that individual judges are independent in the exercise of their powers, and that the judiciary as a whole is independent, its sphere of authority protected from the influence, overt or insidious, of other government actors.[24] But independence of judiciary is an anomaly in the context of countries where rulers decide the outcome of judgment.

No human rights subject will be complete without the mention of a regime that is arguably the most notorious of the highest order in the world—Zimbabwe. Creating a hollow in a judiciary is not mere exhaustion of laws—it is the exhaustion of existing laws to replace new ones in their place to suit the whims of a political party. It makes the leaders appear law-abiding but in truth they use the laws that they shaped to decide the fate of their dissidents. That is exactly what Robert Mugabe, the leader of Zimbabwe, has done.

His government has changed the country's constitution 14 times and passed laws that effectively criminalize peaceful dissent. After two decades of patronage, the police now routinely refuse to enforce court orders the government does not like, or to investigate crimes committed by its supporters.[25] The government is so allergic to foreigners, especially the Westerners, for fear of exposing its misrule such as torture, imprisoning political dissidents, assault as well as arbitrary detention of those it fears, that it has restricted several international food aid programmes despite compelling evidence, according to Amnesty International, of Zimbabwe's impending food shortages.

---

24. Sandra Day O'Connor, *The importance of judicial independence*, 15th September, 2003, http://usinfo.state.gov/journals/itdhr/0304/ijde/oconnor.htm

25. *The Economist*, Cuffed Justice, 19th September, 2002, http://www.economist.com

It is said that if you lose confidence in politicians, you can replace them. If you lose confidence in judges, you still have to live with them. For ordinary Zimbabweans as well as for a few billions around the world struggling under authoritarian rule, everyday living is such that they have to live with foul politics and flawed justice. There is neither sunrise nor is there any sunset for the foreseeable time. They tread in the hazy light of injustice that unjustly and unendingly lingers on.

When political interests flirt with justice, the death knell of judiciary will not be far behind. Human rights cannot possibly flourish amidst politicians who are more communal-ridden than secular, more criminal than honest, more sick than sound and more self-centred than welfare-oriented.

Child labour, Child rights and Globalization

Childhood is the most important stage in the overall development of man. The seed of self-actualization is actually sown in the early stage of childhood with nourishing environment, right education, proper upbringing, wholesome values and healthy habits. Such a privilege does not extend to every child living in this world. Often reality bites, quite harshly, many an unprivileged child who has to toil, suffer ignominy or even taste death without having the privilege to experience the fruits of childhood. Poverty more often than not drags poor children into the callous world of child labour. Child labour is a serious problem affecting "… one in every six children aged 5 to 17 worldwide."[26] Millions of children around the world work full-time under hazardous work conditions facing health risks and danger to their lives.

Child labour is a continuing scourge in the face of humanity. It is an age-old problem that has been inherited for generations by different communities in different societies at different times. It is not a recent occurrence. Yet quite often, it is seen as a product of globalization always intent on exploiting child workers since globalization stands as a byword for economic liberalization and market deregulation which in turn stand for profit-making.

The problem affecting a large number of child workers is not due to lack of human conscience or human propensity to see them suffer in harsh environment. The problem affecting them, in one simple word, is: poverty. Why do children have to work at an age, when they should, like every other child, be playing, singing rhymes and be free of the burden to labour? The answer again is poverty. When a family is poor, the parents have no option other than sending their chil-

26.International Labour Organisation, *Investing in Every Child—An Economic Study of the Costs and Benefits of Eliminating Child Labour*, Foreword, 2004

dren to work in unhygienic, dangerous and foul conditions or they simply send them to beg in the streets. In some depressing cases, hapless young girls are forced or force themselves into prostitution. Other than poverty, there is no other reason why a child should work or be forced to work. No prosperous parents or family would ever wish to see their children roiling in back-breaking labour.

It is easy to take a high moral ground and get incensed at globalization for encouraging child labour since children are forced to plant seeds, manufacture toys, rear cattle, process food packets, wash clothes, clean utensils, carry bricks, do prostitution and every other sort of despicable and menial labour that one could imagine. Our moral anger bellows when we hear or see people in rich countries as well as the rich people in poor countries play with the toys, flaunt their handbags, clothes and shoes, and use other gadgets produced by children wilting under inhuman work conditions in sweatshops and factories. Often they work by sacrificing their childhood. Sad as it is but we often fail to touch the core of the problem in our hustle and bustle to victimize corporations that manufacture the products or vilify the market through which they are sold to the public who happen to buy them. The truth is that globalization—wherever it translates into greater general prosperity and reduced poverty—only accelerates the reduction of child labour and enhances primary school enrolment and hence literacy.[27] Globalization, in effect, has played a vital role in reducing the number of child workers.

When parents are well-off, they tend to have smaller families and invest more in the education and welfare of their children. Western countries are able to largely eradicate child labour due to the economic benefits they were able to reap and sustain over the years. As incomes grow families tend to care better for their children thus reducing the number of children forced to work. The evidence of the impact of rising incomes on child labour is also dramatic. Between 1993 and 1998 income of the poorest 10 percent of Vietnamese rose by more than a half, in real terms. This led to a sharp reduction in child labour (mostly on the family farm) and greater investment in their education.[28] Preventing economic growth would only force the children back into their farms, dirty factories, prostitution and other forms of dangerous occupations which would be far worse.

---

27. Jagdish Bhagwati, *In Defense of Globalization*, (New York, Oxford University Press, 2004), p. 68

28. Martin Wolf, *Why Globalisation Works*, (New Haven and London, Yale NB, 2005), p. 187

What appears an abuse of child rights through globalization or economic development is an illusion since economic growth has brought down the actual number of child workers when the total number of population is taken into consideration. The reason is simple: as families were able to earn more income by way of increasing number of jobs, through 'predatory' private corporations both national and foreign, they also have been able to step out of poverty. Hence, parents were able to do away with the income generated by their children through hard physical labour. Professor Eric Edmonds at Dartmouth College in the U.S., in a paper[29] on the relation between child labour and economic growth, interprets data from 1993 to 1997 studying over 3,000 Vietnamese families, to emphasize that GDP growth per head reduces the number of children toiling on the labour terrain. Edmonds concludes in his paper that improvement in economic status is the cause of decline in child labour and that in Vietnamese families "… per capita expenditure improvements can explain 80 percent of the observed decline in child labour."[30] Experience, thus, shows poverty as the cause of forcing children into work rather than into the portals of education. It is again poverty that destroys the flowering of childhood instead of letting the free spirit of a child take wings. The link between child labour and globalization is weak and diametrically inconsistent to experience despite which some anti-market, anti-trade and anti-globalization renegades would want us believe otherwise.

For many, especially, in the rich countries it has become almost a fad to rile against child labour because it is rather easy for them to compare their living standards they and their children enjoy against those they see in the developing world. They often fail to see the improvement in the lives of the poor in developing countries.

Experience in the rich countries show that government pressures did not wipe out child labour completely until when families could afford to part with the income brought in by their child workers. In the 19th century Britain, the ordeal of child labour was so funereal that, "the youngest children in the textile factories were usually employed as scavengers and piercers; … most factories were dirty; low-roofed; ill-ventilated; ill-drained; no conveniences for washing or dressing; no contrivance for carrying off dust and other effluvia; … children constantly complained about the quality of the food. In most textile mills the children had to eat their meals while still working. This meant that the food tended to get cov-

---

29.Eric V. Edmonds, *Does child labour decline with improving economic status?*
     The Journal of Human Resources 40 (1), Winter 2005, 77–99
     30.ibid

ered with the dust from the cloth; ... Children were usually hit with a strap to make them work faster. In some factories children were dipped head first into the water cistern if they became drowsy. Children were also punished for arriving late for work and for talking to the other children; ... unguarded machinery was a major problem for children working in factories. One hospital reported that every year it treated nearly a thousand people for wounds and mutilations caused by machines in factories. A report commissioned by the House of Commons in 1832 said that: "there are factories, no means few in number, nor confined to the smaller mills, in which serious accidents are continually occurring, and in which, notwithstanding, dangerous parts of the machinery are allowed to remain unfenced."[31]

The truth that rich countries attained their wealthy status through what today's developing countries do—employing child workers—is no justification that a nation should build its economic edifice on the crumbling fragility of childhood labour. The point is that some leaders, anti-global activists and anarchists in rich countries deliberately or ignorantly fail to see the way their countries developed in their one-dimensional obsession to eliminate child labour. Often, they fail to see the larger picture. Child labour is outlawed in many rich countries today. Since child labour is no longer an issue in rich countries, a high moral ground is held to sermonize poor countries to abolish child labour while the proponents of anti-child labour jump on the bandwagon with their eyes shut on reality.

In the context of India, which constitutes the world's largest number of child workers, Article 45 of the Constitution of India proclaims provision for free and compulsory education for children. The Article declares that "The State shall endeavour to provide, within a period of ten years form the commencement of this Constitution, for free and compulsory education for all children until they complete the age of fourteen years". Even 50 years after the framing of the Constitution, India has not been able to make a significant dent in the reduction of child labour until recently when the country integrated with the global economy.

Despite being home to the world's largest number of child labourers those Indian states, which actively embraced globalization have significantly managed to reduce the total number of their child workers. Going by the statistics of India's Ministry of Labour, the major states have seen a drop in the number of working children in the age group 5–14 years.

---

31. Spartacus Educational, *Child Labour, Life in the factory*, http://www.spartacus.schoolnet.co.uk/IRchild.main.htm

According to the Census data on Child Labour published by India's Ministry of Labour, the total number of child workers was about 13.6 million in 1981 which went down to 11.2 million in 1991 but has since increased to 12.6 million in 2001. All the big states (See Table 1) of India with the exception of Delhi and West Bengal have successfully whittled down the number of child workers. The States such as Andhra Pradesh, Gujarat, Karnataka, Tamil Nadu, and Maharashtra have seen a drop in the number of their child labourers through better exploitation of globalization and curtailment of their population growth. The only exceptions, apart from the poorer states, are Delhi and West Bengal where the number of child labourers has increased. They deserve an explanation. In the case of Delhi, the city has seen an explosive growth in its population. Delhi has been growing at about 1,000 persons per day (350,000 per annum) for a number of years,[32] including migration from other parts of the neighbouring states. Needless to emphasize, the neighbouring states of Delhi are comparatively a lot poorer than Delhi. The annual growth rate of population of Delhi during 1991–2001 has been recorded as 3.85 percent and it is almost double the national average[33] and according the Registrar General & Census Commissioner statistics the decadal growth for Delhi rose from 9.4 million during 1981–1991 to 13.8 million at a whopping "… 46.31 (percent) during the decade 1991–2001."[34] West Bengal too has seen a massive population explosion from 68 million in 1991 to 80 million in 2001, according to the State Government's census,[35] but the State's communist adherence meant the failure to exploit the benefits of globalization as well as an increase in the state's child workers.

32. ASHA, Delhi Municipal Administration, http://www.asha-india.org
33. Planning Department, Economic Survey of Delhi 2003–2004, Chapter 3, *Demographic Profile*, p18
34. Census of India, 2001 Results by States, Registrar General & Census Commissioner—India, For more information visit, http://www.censusindia.net/profiles/
35. Population and its growth, West Bengal 1991–2001, http://www.wbgov.com

State-wise Distribution of Working Children according to 1971, 1981, 1991 and 2001 Census in the age group 5–14 years

Name of the State	Year 1971	Year 1981	Year 1991	Year 2001
Andhra Pradesh	1,627,492	1,951,312	1,661,940	1,363,339
Delhi	**17,120**	**25,717**	**27,351**	**41,899**
Gujarat	518,061	616,913	523,585	485,530
Karnataka	808,719	1,131,530	976,247	822,615
Tamil Nadu	713,305	975,055	578,889	418,801
West Bengal	**511,443**	**605,263**	**711,691**	**857,087**
Total	*4,196,140*	*5,305,790*	*4,479,703*	*3,989,271*

Table 1: Census of Child Workers' population in India during the four decades from 1971–2001.
For more statistical information, visit the Ministry of Labour, Government of India. http://labour.nic.in/cwl/ChildLabour.htm

The fact that India's total number of child workers has reduced must be seen in the light of the number of workers against the country's growth in population. Table 2 reveals the down slide in the number of child workers in terms of percentage against a rapidly growing general population of the country. Reaching a conclusion solely on the extent of growth of child labourers often leads to misinterpretation of numbers when the growth in general population through birth as well as migration is ignored. From the figures cited it is clear that even though the number of child workers has increased the percentage of total number of child workers, in the face of India's population growth, has diminished.

Year	General Population	Total Number of Child Workers	Percentage of Child Workers
1971	548,159,652	10,753,985	1.96
1981	683,329,097	13,640,870	1.99
1991	846,302,688	11,285,349	1.33
2001	1,027,015,247	12,666,377	1.23

Table 2: Total Number of Child Workers against decadal growth of general population General Population figures taken from www.censusindia.net; Child Workers statistics taken from Ministry of Labour, Government of India, http://labour.nic.in

Child labour is not just a slap in the face of human civility but also a shameful blot on societies. Nevertheless, it is only through globalization and by helping the developing world to integrate more into the global economy that the fruits of globalization can be dispersed to the poverty-ridden people in poor countries. But that will not offer a quick-fix solution nor will their betterment be expedient. Where more globalization will be beneficial for eradicating child labour in the long term is through increased direct foreign investment in developing countries, helping poor countries to integrate with the wider global community so as to help them boost their exports and increase their foreign reserves as well as assisting them in importing and acquiring advanced techniques and skills, improving labour productivity and creating more jobs. Globalization has already proved successful in diminishing the number of child labourers around the world. A recent report entitled, "The end of child labour—Within reach', produced under the International Labour Organization's (ILO) Declaration of Fundamental Principles and Rights at Work and the International Programme on the Elimination of Child Labour (IPEC), says we are beginning to see an encouraging sign in the reduction of worldwide child labour. The more weighty fact is its statement that if current trends continue, child labour in its worst forms may be wiped out in the next decade.

The report indicates that the number of child labourers globally has fallen by 11 percent over the last four years—or 28 million fewer than 2002. The sharpest decrease is in the area of hazardous work by children—where there has been a 26 percent reduction overall, and 33 percent fewer children between the ages of 5 and 14 endangering their lives in hazardous work.[36]

While multinational corporations have created several jobs in the recent years in several developing countries that with a more conducive environment in several backward and poor countries there is scope for more stable and remunerative employment. By redirecting the benefits of globalization towards the lower economic strata of societies and political will matched with right policies there is a tremendous scope to relieve poverty-hit families of their need to push their children to work. In the long term, as more developing countries adapt to a globalizing economy they stand to whittle down the number of child labourers going to work.

---

36. International Labour Conference, *The end of child labour—Within reach*, Global Report under the follow-up to the ILO Declaration on Fundamental Principles and Rights at work, Report to the International Labour Conference, 95th Session, 2006

CHAPTER 5

▼

THE COMPLEXITY OF ENVIRONMENT

The concerns emanating from environmental degradation leading to the harming of the planet have assumed gargantuan proportions. Several reasons are attributed to the impairment of the environment ranging from man's insatiable greed for economic growth to man's materialistic infatuation with his unrelenting chase for profit and luxury. Calls for placing a cap on man's indiscriminate consumption of material goods and on the blinding pace of exploitation of natural resources to dilute the world's growing obsession with economic riches, keep untiringly emerging to the fore—all at the expense of environmental stability. Voices frequently erupt in different parts of the world as to how best we could, and should, tackle the growing heat and dust of the environmental challenge.

Seldom have environmentalists and economists agreed on issues affecting both people and the planet. Environmentalists incriminate economists for their reckless extravagance, greed, and seeming detachment from green issues. The economists, in turn, counter charge the ecologists' irrational paranoia over economic growth, which has brought phenomenal prosperity to hundreds of millions of poor people around the world and a qualitative change in the standard of living of millions of people across the world. The fear over the expeditious use of energy resources as developing economies press themselves for higher economic growth, and the worry about environmental pollution along with the warming of the planet, have contributed to the alarm of survival of mankind should we choose to neglect the portending environmental dangers.

The argument that more environmental protection will contribute to more economic ruin runs strong among economists and growth-oriented conservatives. Doubtless, the world today is a lot better than what it was during the medieval times when European travellers such as Christopher Columbus, Ferdinand Magellan, and Vasco da Gama circumnavigated the earth in search of wealth during the 15th and 16th centuries. The world, since then, has dramatically transformed beyond whatever people at the time could have possibly envisioned or imagined in their wildest dreams. Fast forward to the world of today—it is palpable and indisputable that the advance of technology has played a central role in the transformation of our lifestyle, radically and absolutely.

The explorers, spurred by the curiosity to know about foreign lands, foreign people, as well as to find valuable items some 300 or 400 years ago, travelled in search of valued goods such as silk, spices, and even opiates. Modern man is no different from his predecessors in the sense that he is driven by the same instinct to explore and exploit.

Man, from time immemorial, has always travelled, carrying with him not just his paraphernalia but also his ideas to wherever he migrated. At the same time, his curiosity has inspired him to know and learn about his fellow human beings. That inquisitiveness has given way to innovation, creativity, and development of knowledge and skill—thus contributing, generation after generation, to the present state of modern man.

In the last 400 years or so, humanity, globally, has seen revolutions aplenty—political, social, and technological. Political revolutions have chopped and changed governments as different forms of governments and ideologies have surfaced and submerged. Social revolutions have shaped and reshaped human standards of 'life' and 'living'. But, of all the changes, the technological revolutions have had the greatest impact on mankind. The industrial revolution replaced handicraft with machinery, factories and mills; the steam revolution gave birth to steam energy thereby revolutionizing travel by rail; then the steel and electricity revolution transformed economies into massive engineering and electrification; while the manufacturing revolution heralded the championing of automotive industries. In our own time, the digital revolution has brought with it the microprocessor, culminating in what we, today, call revolution in 'information and communications technology' (ICT). At every stage of human development, human society has progressed through layer upon layer of technological revolution.

Human progress, through its various stages of development, did not happen on its own. It involved the consumption of various resources from 'manufactured' energy to available 'natural' capital such as air, water and land. In the process, the platform laid by our predecessors has shaped and reshaped our modern lifestyle endlessly. Ranging from the basic amenities, comforts, and luxuries we enjoy, to the life-saving drugs we take for granted are things made or derived from products of nature. People today, live longer, eat healthier food, and are better sheltered. Scientific and technological progress underpin the discovery of medicines and the invention of drugs to cure deadly diseases and incommodious infections, about which many of our ancestors had no clue and to which several of them perished mysteriously.

Human adeptness to evolve through technology has doubtless brought unimaginable benefits to humankind. On the flip side, it has also created 'unpleasant' corollaries, altering the very environment on which man depends for his continuing life. The corollaries are, in economic jargon, called 'externalities' which are the side effects of one's actions that may affect another person or entity—either positively or negatively. For example, a restoration of a worn-out painting may create a 'positive' externality to a connoisseur of art who benefits by the mere sight of the painting, whereas a nuclear power plant, whilst benefiting its owners, creates a negative 'externality' in the form of radioactive waste which subsequently affects the environment and its inhabitants.

Likewise, in the march towards prosperity and progress, and in an endeavour to respond to the many challenges arising between man and nature, man and man, as well as between man and himself, mankind has created an inestimable amount of 'externalities' during his sojourn on planet 'earth'. Some of the externalities, either directly or indirectly, have contributed to the deteriorating health of the planet. Whether it is the depletion of resources through human consumption of energy or the pollution of air/water/land, or the warming of the planet through emission of poisonous greenhouse gases—the environment, at the present juncture, seems to be undergoing serious changes. Simply put, the health of the environment is far from pleasant. The challenges that humanity are currently facing are indeed formidable.

The biggest challenge, though, lies in finding a balance between growing global needs, tackling pollution, and controlling global warming—without letting the poor slip further away into poverty. In other words, addressing environmental concerns without jeopardizing global economic prosperity is the greatest challenge facing humanity at present.

Energy-dependent man

Energy is an essential part of our life. Our everyday work requires energy. Energy lights up our cities, offices and homes. It brings us pictures on our television sets. It dries our clothes; washes our dishes; cleans our homes. It provides power to our cars, our trains and our planes. The food we eat, the music we listen to or the games we play—use the energy which forms an integral part of our lives. Prior to the discovery of sophisticated forms of energy, man used various basic forms.

Man also used animals as a source of energy to plough land and for transportation. Even human slaves were used as substitutes for energy to do such jobs as carrying people, washing, cleaning and so on. Construction of huts, making cooking utensils or even making a decorative ornament was not possible without expending some amount of energy. Hard physical labour used to be the order of the olden days. It still is in many parts of the world where machinery is a luxury and where electric and electronic gadgets are no more than a dream.

Long before man learned to read or write, he discovered fire for cooking and heating purposes. Fire provided energy. Fire helped man temper his tools to hardness and durability. It helped him eat many things that were previously inedible. It helped him in scaring animals away. It brought him light in darkness and at once, he was to become greatly independent of sunlight.

Undoubtedly, fire is one of humanity's greatest inventions but fire always needed a fuel for its sustenance to provide energy. Wood fulfilled that void and for a long time it served as the prime fuel. But man's increasing desire for energy drastically changed when James Watt invented a commercially viable steam engine. Steam fuelled the Industrial Revolution in the 18th century. It was an economy dependent on steam when "steam engine", "steam boat" and "steam locomotive" were the engines of economic prosperity powered by coal. From the mid eighteenth century to the mid-nineteenth century coal reigned supreme as it was the major fuel for power plants and industry.

The onset of modern oil use started in the 19th century with the drilling of the first commercial oil well in the year 1858. The advent of oil revolutionized global economic outlook, triggering massive industrial growth, transforming travel, improving family lifestyle and redefining business operations. Today, oil has come to quench the global thirst for energy needs. The discovery of natural gas is a bonus to the established resources of coal and oil. Natural gas was first used for illumination, primarily in gas street lights, in 1785 in Britain, and in 1816 in the United States. The first natural gas well was built in 1821 in Fredonia, New York and, in 1859, natural gas was first produced in the United States on an industrial basis.[1] However, of all the fossil fuels, oil has come to occupy the heart of human activity. Both the industrialized as well as the newly industrializing countries, mainly China, India and Brazil, have come to depend heavily on oil as their economies grow. Consumption of energy, in the current fervent global economic activity, is practically unavoidable.

Coal, oil and natural gas are collectively known as fossil fuels. They are all the products of dead plants and animals buried, left, and decomposed under the earth for hundreds of millions of years. Coal used to be an indispensable energy-producing asset. Though coal is still used widely in many countries, its usage has drastically reduced. The energy in coal comes from giant plants that died in swamps some 300 million years ago, when the earth was greatly swamped with forests. Over several millennia, a layer of perished plants at the base of the swamps was swaddled by further layers of water and dirt, drawing the energy of the dead plants. Under heat and pressure, the perished plants underwent numerous chemical and physical changes, eventually forming a blackish, solid fuel— and this is what we know as coal. Oil and natural gas, however, are composed of sea plants and animals which died and were buried under the sea floor some 300–400 million years ago. Over millions of years, as the remains of dead plants and animals got buried deeper and deeper, the immense heat and pressure turned them into oil and gas. Using modern technology, oil and gas deposits are extracted from the rock formations under the sea by drilling down through layers of sand, silt and rock.

Modern civilization is extremely reliant on an adequate supply of energy resources—particularly the finite resources that are incapable of replacement once they are fully used up. Their replacement rate is decisively slow, ranging in millions of years since the energy resources—oil, coal and gas—that we primarily consume today were accumulated over millions of years. The most important question is whether we can sustain our dependency on such dying resources.

It is argued that in our mindless hunt for wealth and material prosperity we are consuming millions of years of energy resources in a matter of few hundred years. Not surprisingly, free markets and trade are readily vilified by environmentalists and activists alike. At any rate, conservation of non-renewable resources is not going to stop their depletion. That is the hard and bitter truth. Even if the world used just one barrel of oil a year this would still imply that some future

---

1. dKosopedia, the free political encyclopedia, *History of Energy*, http://www.dkosopedia.com/wiki/History_of_Energy

generation would be left with no oil at all.[2] The challenge currently facing humanity is not mainly about how to conserve and prevent depletion of non-renewable resources but how efficiently we use current availability of resources and how quickly we are able to develop other renewable sources of energy through technology and human expertise.

Much of the contention doing rounds in the energy circles is about whether we have enough energy upon which we build our economic prosperity. The answer is that we will not run out of energy, mainly fossil fuels, in the foreseeable future. As various forms of renewable energy sources are being developed at various stages the future does not seem as dire as it is often portrayed to be. There are, of course, hitches and hurdles in ensuring a seamless supply of fossil fuels, and in developing renewable energy sources which offer opportunities for mankind to nurture and develop with its technical ingenuity.

Oil—the Myth and the Reality

Like any other fossil fuel, oil is finite. Hence, only a certain amount of it is available and it is not renewable unlike any other product of energy such as solar power or wind power. Therefore, oil, in that regard, becomes valuable as its availability is limited by its finiteness. The precious black gold, as oil is popularly known, has been an elixir of economic prosperity while at the same time remaining a commodity—instigating instability in the Middle East and a cause of contention between America and the Middle East. Setting aside oil's political dimension, it has been the most sought-after commodity. The increasing demand for oil, particularly in the developing world and especially China and India as they progress economically, has never been fiercer and greater. Oil is the most attractive fuel compared to coal and gas. Because of its tendency to pollute the environment and its heaviness, coal has least attractiveness. Gas, though clean, is bulky and requires pipelines for transportation. The fact that oil has versatility and high-energy content is why it is priced dearer than other fossil fuels.

Gloom merchants have been predicting the evanescence of oil resulting from the global obsession with "economic growth" and its impetuous preoccupation with "materialism". The pessimists bellow that we are on the verge of an energy breakdown. The optimists holler that total depletion of oil is still many decades away. The arguments have already created enough mist blocking the way to contrive a solution. It is obvious that the commodity in question is certain to deplete

---

2. Bjørn Lomborg, *The Skeptical Environmentalist*, (Cambridge, Cambridge University Press, 2001), p. 119

at some point of time in the future. It makes little sense to haggle over whether it is going to last for one hundred and sixty years or one hundred and eighty years.

Scarcity of oil occurs not just through its depletion but also due to political bickering. The world has experienced several bouts of oil crisis through political crises threatening the supply of oil. The first oil shock came in 1973 during the Arab-Israeli war, prompting many Arab countries to stop shipping oil to the United States and other countries sympathetic to Israel. The second shock ensued upon the ousting of the Shah of Iran during the Iranian Revolution of 1979 as oil shipments to the United States came to a stop. But the bigger shock at the time came when OPEC (Organization of Petroleum Exporting Countries) doubled its prices. The third oil shock arrived when Iraq invaded Kuwait in 1990, forcing the United States and coalition forces to expel Iraq out of Kuwait. During the political upheavals there were surging demands for oil and prices shot up as a result of constricted supply of oil. The oil crisis happened because during the 1970's and the beginning of the 1980's the OPEC countries were able to cut back production and squeeze up prices. But, it was never an indication of an actual scarcity.[3] The scarcity arose out of political polemics, not out of oil wells' scantiness.

Beyond political determinants of oil supply, fears always abound as to the impending end of supply of cheap oil threatening human civilization. M. King Hubbert, a Shell Oil Company geologist, predicted half a century ago that global oil production would face an irreversible decline around year 2000. In contrary to his prediction, "global oil production in 2003 was about 2.5 percent above 2000."[4] The world is never scarce of unascertained worries. In 1972, a popular book, The Limits to Growth was published, which attracted widespread acclaim for the heap of environmental anguish it managed to generate and for the "irresponsible rubbish,"[5] it produced. The book made numerous predictions, claiming that man would soon run out of many resources: gold would run out in 1981, silver and mercury in 1985, zinc in 1990, petroleum in 1992, and copper, lead,

---

3. ibid, p. 120
4. Robert L Bradley Jr, *Are we running out of oil?* PERC (Property and Environment Research Center,
   http://www.perc.org
5. Henry C Wallich, a Yale economist, called the book 'Limits to Growth' as "a piece of irresponsible nonsense" in his 13th March, 1972 Newsweek editorial

and natural gas by 1993."[6] Though the predictions never materialized, the fears whipped up in the pages of the book were of colossal magnitude.

Many oil pundits in the past have got predictions of oil receding from its wells wrong. One of the reasons has been the paucity of information about, and incorrect forecasting of, oil reserves in many parts of the world. Large tracts of fields are still left unexplored. Exxon says it has learned one crucial lesson from earlier forecasting mistakes: it greatly underestimated the power of technology. Thanks to advances in exploration and production technology, the amount of oil available has increased enormously.[7] There are strong reasons not to panic when a sense of disquiet emerges out of thinning oil supply for we do not know the lifetime of existing reserves nor the possibility of exploration discovering new oil reserves.

The planet is vast. There are practical difficulties in knowing all the places richly endowed with oil. Yet, given human ingenuity to explore more oil fields, the feasibility of identifying new oil fields remains high. In 2002, the US Geological Survey (USGS) completed an assessment of the undiscovered conventional oil and gas potential of 128 of the world's petroleum provinces. Of the eight global regions studied by the USGS, the Arabian Peninsula portion of the Middle East region was estimated to contain the greatest volumes of undiscovered oil and gas. Moreover, the USGS estimates a mean of (undiscovered) 37 billion barrels of oil and 808 trillion cubic feet of gas.[8]

Looking at the graduation of usage of different types of energy it is obvious that humanity continually explored different options. From using wood to animals to humans to coal to oil and gas, human expertise to exploit resources cannot be underestimated. Contrary to what was predicted by 'experts' about disappearance of oil, advance of technology has enabled more extraction of oil from existing oil reserves. Currently available technology sucks only about 30–35 percent of oil from the reservoir. Industry optimists believe that new techniques on the drawing board today could lift that figure to 50–60 percent within a decade.[9]

---

6. Bill Emmott, *20:21 Vision, The Lessons of the 20th Century for the 21st*, (London, Penguin, 2004), p. 243

7. *The Economist*, Will the oil run out? Survey: Energy, 8th February, 2001, http://www.economist.com

8. USGS, *Undiscovered Oil and Gas Resources of Lower Silurian Qusaiba-Paleosoic Total Petroleum Systems*, Arabian Peninsula, January 2002, http://pubs.usgs.gov/fs/fs-0008–02/

9. *The Economist*, Sunset for the oil business? 1st November, 2001, http://www.economist.com

Benefits of progress in technology through economic growth have minimized the pressure for greater oil consumption. Modern cars have better engine performance; their engine power has increased by roughly 30 percent as engineering and development techniques have improved. The efficiency of production of modern cars is a sterling example of conforming to environmental standards. For instance in the US, the total number of car-miles travelled has more than doubled over the past 30 years. The economy has likewise more than doubled, and the population has increased by more than a third. Nevertheless, over the same period emissions have decreased by a third and concentrations of emissions much more.[10]

Consumption of lubrication oil has gone down by nearly 60 percent, with much longer periods now between service intervals and oil changes. Besides this, technological progress has made modern appliances such as refrigerators, dishwashers, washing machines and even light bulbs consume less energy. These are indications of more efficient exploitation of resources. The possibility of alternative sources of energy—such as solar, wind, geothermal, biomass, hydro, and ocean—offer hope that the singular dependency of man on non-renewable energy commodities will subside without much ado. Currently, renewable energy sources contribute only a little part of our daily energy needs. Over time, renewable energy sources will provide a major chunk of our energy requirements.

Oil fears are enormously exaggerated. Should any such doubt exist, then Al-Shaybah, an oil field in Saudi Arabia is the antidote. The kingdom's vast oil reserves are not past their prime. "(Al)-Shaybah can pump (oil) at a rate of 600,000 barrels a day for 70 years, and that's without replacing any reserves,"[11] according to Hussain al-Obaid, Al-Shaybah's engineering superintendent. Al-Shaybah opens wider possibilities of extracting more oil if it could explore and develop a few more oil fields. Oil may be on the road to extinction tomorrow, but it offers immense opportunities to go a long way today. The discovery of fossil fuels is a recent phenomenon even though prophets of doom wail as if humans were born along with oil and gas at birth. Humanity existed and lived even before the discovery of fossil fuels. As it is important to explore alternative sources of energy, we should not hypocritically behave as if we were entitled by some divine power to live with finite fossil fuels for time infinite.

10.Bjørn Lomborg, p. 177

11.*Forbes*, Shaybah shows proof of Saudi oilfield stamina, 3rd September, 2004, http://www.forbes.com

Natural Gas and Coal—Possibilities and Challenges

Natural gas is cleaner than other fossil fuels. It has fewer emissions of sulphur, carbon and nitrogen than coal or oil. Due to its reputation as a clean fuel, the use of natural gas has grown in demand. As with any other fuel, there are environmental concerns with gas producing carbon dioxide—the most important greenhouse gas. Nevertheless, natural gas is one of the cleanest sources of energy and a lot cleaner than coal. The demand for natural gas is reflected in the face of increasing global consumption of goods and services and worldwide economic growth. In 1980, the demand for natural gas was 53 trillion cubic feet and in 2002, it reached 92 trillion cubic feet. According to Energy Information Administration, from 2003 to 2030, the natural gas share of total world energy consumption is projected to increase from 24 (percent) in 2003 to 26 percent in 2030, while the consumption of natural gas worldwide is set to increase from 95 trillion cubic feet in 2003 to 182 trillion cubic feet in 2030.[12] Historically, world natural gas reserves have, for the most part, trended upward. As of January 1, 2006, proven world natural gas reserves were estimated at 6,112 trillion cubic feet—70 trillion cubic feet (about 1 percent) higher than the estimate for 2005.[13]

Despite the fact that the world's gas reserves are by far more widely dispersed than the oil fields the possibility of Liquefied Natural Gas (LNG) being transported to remote areas safely and securely has only remained slight. The costs associated with liquefying, transporting and re-gasifying have been huge. But, with the costs of oil shooting upwards and being volatile, energy investors have started to show more interest in LNG. Besides the desire to diversify fuel sources in order to improve energy security, the pressure from environmental lobbies, and to meet the targets set by the Kyoto protocol to reduce greenhouse-gas emissions, the interest in the revival of LNG has become more pronounced.

One way to exploit this opportunity is through developing and handling LNG in a much more cost-effective way. The biggest hindrance to optimizing the exploitation of liquefied natural gas is its transportation and storage. This could be overcome "… by cooling it to–161°C (thus reducing) its volume by 600-fold. It can then be transported by sea in specially built tankers and reconverted to gas at the point where it enters an importer's pipeline system. This is a costly investment, but then so is laying a pipeline. According to America's Gas Technology

12. Energy Information Administration, *International Energy Outlook 2006*, June 2006, http://www.eia.doe.gov/oiaf/ieo/nat_gas.html
13. ibid

Institute, liquefying gas, shipping and then re-gasifying it is cheaper than sending it by undersea pipeline over distances of more than 700 miles, or 2,200 miles in the case of overland pipelines."[14]

A huge bulk of gas, that is more than 90 percent of global gas consumption, is delivered by pipeline. Even though new and massive gas fields are being discovered regularly, their utilization is often hampered by geographical constraints such as oceans dividing countries, as well as their presence in politically unstable countries. By including the economic restrictions placed upon foreign ownership and investment in developing the potential of LNG, Russia and Iran, despite having largest reserves of natural gas in the world, pose difficulties in the exploitation of LNG. While Russia places restrictions on foreign participation in extracting mineral resources, Iran, through its constitution, prevents foreign ownership within the country's oil sector, which technically rules out any kind of production-sharing agreement with foreign oil companies interested in gas exploration.

The situation though is not as bleak as it may seem. Qatar, with its huge natural gas reserves and also the third largest in the world, has opened the sector to foreign investment. Qatar is trying to become the world's largest principal LNG supplier. When Royal Dutch/Shell signed a $7 billion project deal with Qatar's state-owned gas company—Qatar Petroleum—to produce 7.5 million tonnes of LNG per year, the Second Deputy Premier and Minister of Energy and Industry of Qatar, Abdullah bin Hamad Al-Attiyah said that Qatar's goal was "to be the world's leader in LNG"[15] and "further contribute to the diversification of LNG markets."[16] Exxon Mobil, an American company, too signed a much bigger deal, "... valued at $12.8 billion"[17] to produce "... 15.8 million metric tons of LNG."[18] The deals were significant as they underlined the big swell of interest in LNG.

Political instability and unwillingness of governments to invite foreign investment are bound to continue but since gas reserves are distributed widely, oil firms

---

14. *The Economist*, The natural-gas explosion, 28th February, 2005, http://www.economist.com

15. Shell, *Qatar Petroleum and Shell sign a Heads of Agreement for the development of Qatargas 4—a large scale LNG project*, Press Release, 27th February, 2005, www.shell.com

16. ibid

17. Market Watch, *Qatar gives big boost to LNG trade*, Feb 28, 2005, www.marketwatch.com

18. ibid

need not solely depend on countries such as Russia and Iran. Countries like Qatar, which are more willing to slash red tape and bureaucracy and are open to foreign investment, show that the prospect of exploration and exploitation of natural gas has not dimmed yet.

Coal, historically, has been an important source of energy. It was briefly displaced in its wider application by the sudden emergence of oil. In the affluent years after the (Second World) war, as natural gas and fuel oil became more available, people turned away from coal, scrapping their big stoves, dusty furnaces, and ash cans forever.[19] The fall of coal from grace did not last very long.

The energy crisis in the 1970's saw the return of coal. Coal is still widely used in many countries around the world today and still remains an enormously important fuel and is the largest single source of electricity worldwide. In the United States, for example, the burning of coal generates 50% of the electricity consumed.[20] The abundant presence of coal reserves is widely distributed around the world. Estimates of the world's total recoverable reserves of coal in 2002 were about 1,081 billion short tons. The resulting ratio of coal reserves to production exceeds 200 years, meaning that at current rates of production (and no change in reserves), coal reserves could in theory last for another two centuries.[21]

Coal represents an option to supply energy for a long time to come. The downside with coal is its polluting nature. Coal is responsible for large part of carbon dioxide emissions; it is the exclusive producer of the so-called 'greenhouse gases' and it causes respiratory disease. Coal-fired plants generate twice the amount of carbon-dioxide per unit of electricity generated compared to natural gas-fired plants. Of all the contributors to global warming power generation industries occupy the largest share, and coal is the biggest culprit of all. Coal-fired plants are responsible for perhaps 8 billion out of the 28 billion tonnes of man-made carbon dioxide released every year, and are thus a prime target for emissions cuts.[22]

19. Barbara Freese, *Coal—A Human History*, (London, Arrow, 2005), p. 160

20. Wikipedia, the free encyclopedia, *Coal*, http://en.wikipedia.org/wiki/Coal#World_coal_reserves

21. Energy Information Administration, Energy Information Sheets Index, *Coal Reserves*, August 2004, http://www.eia.doe.gov/neic/infosheets/coalreserves.htm

22. *The Economist*, Can coal be clean? Technology Quarterly, 2nd December, 2006, p. 30

Despite its availability and toxic nature, coal provides a bit of promise. Tighter environmental regulations can actually spur the need to develop new ways to reduce mercury emissions from coal-burning power plants. The coal industry has come up with ways to reduce sulphur, nitrogen oxides and other pollutants from coal. Power plants use "scrubbers" to clean sulphur from the smoke before it leaves their smokestacks. In addition, there is a mass of research into such ideas (of producing clean coal energy), much of it, as in Canada and Australia, powered by a joint get-together of the big coal-users and government.[23] The good sign is, sooner rather than later, coal could be a lot cleaner and certainly more profitable.

Nuclear Energy—still mired in uncertainties

The word 'nuclear' often just raises hair among world's politicians and ruffles provocative bristles between the 'growth-minded' economists and the 'green-sensitive' environmentalists. Amidst growing despair of 'dwindling' fossil fuels, nuclear energy—when the first nuclear power plant was opened in England in 1956—was seen as a salvation. In contrast to the finite supply of coal, oil, and gas and as a result of its less polluting characteristic, as an upshot of its ability to produce immense quantity of energy, nuclear energy came to serve as a sturdy option for an energy-guzzling humanity. Nuclear energy assumes more importance because it serves as a realistic substitute for oil, gas and coal despite some looming uncomfortable questions.

Until the recent past, the debate on nuclear energy was about how to retire existing nuclear reactors gracefully. The debate now has taken a different road. Today, it is not merely about how to revive the existing reactors but also about constructing new ones. As of 1st April 2006, there were about 443 nuclear power plants in operation and 26 nuclear power plants under construction worldwide.[24]

As China and India grow their economies up the demand for energy is only set to increase manifold. China already has 9 nuclear reactors up and running while India is running 15 fully functioning ones while "France generates 78 percent of

23. *The Economist*, The future is clean, 2nd September, 2004,
    http://www.economist.com
24. International Atomic Energy Agency, *Nuclear power and sustainable development*, 2006,
    http://www.iaea.org/Publications/Booklets/Development/npsd0506.pdf

its electricity through its 59 reactors."[25] A host of several other countries still remain gleefully cosy with the tenability of nuclear energy.

A sense of assurance is sweeping across the nuclear terrain—partly because of the improvement in the efficiency of modern nuclear reactors and partly due to optimism that nuclear reactors can get better with advances in technology. The modern rectors, also known as third generation reactors, are more efficient than their predecessors—they possess the standardized design to minimize capital cost and construction time; longer working life; reduced possibility of meltdown accidents; economical fuel use and generate less amounts of nuclear waste.

The overhanging sense of optimism about what is called the 'fourth generation' (Generation IV) nuclear reactors—a much improved version of the third— promise to deliver much more. The fourth generation reactors are set to be "highly economical" with an "enhanced safety" design that will "minimize wastes" and be "proliferation restraint" though they are not expected to be fully functional at least until 2030.

Attentively nurtured under the aegis of The Generation IV International Forum (GIF), the development of Generation IV nuclear reactors is a ten-nation research programme comprising Argentina, Brazil, Canada, France, Japan, South Africa, South Korea, Switzerland, the United Kingdom and the United States. A typically futuristic reactor, it has an innate safety feature that will allow the reactor to 'breakdown' safely. The safe 'breakdown' feature is the ability of a reactor to shut itself down automatically should its control systems cease working. It then allows the heat, produced by the reactions in its core, to dissipate without causing any hazard. It also prevents the escape of fuel and radioactive waste by putting them away in some form of receptacle.[26]

Asian countries have always had a feeling of warmth towards 'nuclear energy'—a sentiment not widely shared by the European countries. For over two decades, European countries endeavoured to do away with nuclear energy, especially those countries in the Scandinavian region where environmental concerns had always ruled the political roost. Sweden abandoned nuclear energy altogether. Finland's parliament delivered a thumping rejection when TVO, a utility company, presented an application in 1993 to build a nuclear plant. In politics as well as in technology nothing remains static for a long time. After twelve years of hibernation, interest in nuclear energy revved up in Finland. In 2005, ironically,

25. Kavin Kanagasabai, *Nuclear-still unclear*, www.se7enmagazine.org, Issue 54, August 5–17, 2006
26. ibid

amidst environmental and energy worries, the Finnish demonstrated that they were not finished with nuclear energy yet. TVO this time was granted permission to build an EPR (European Pressurized Reactor) nuclear plant in the town of Olkiluoto with the help of a French state-owned company, Areva, costing $3.6 billion.[27]

The EPR is the world's first third-generation reactor comprising several active and passive protection measures against accidents. The EPR comprises four independent emergency cooling systems, each capable of cooling down the reactor should it fail; a solid leak-tight container built around the reactor; a containment to prevent the escape of molten core from the reactor and a two-layered concrete wall to withstand the collision of an airplane or terrorist attack. Areva is a one-stop nuclear shop whose activities range from mining and enriching uranium ore to making nuclear fuel, designing and constructing nuclear reactors, providing expertise to operating them, and to recycling spent fuel. The company also entered into a joint venture with an American company, Constellation Energy based in Baltimore, to build an advanced nuclear power plant. Encouraged by the prospects of EPR, France evinced keenness in building a similar reactor in Flamanville subject to it getting through public scrutiny.[28]

The hazardous political realities of Middle Eastern countries have spurred several countries to look into the possibilities of generating energy independently. For instance Japan, with 90 percent of its oil coming from the Middle East, is reconsidering its heavy reliance on the crisis-prone Middle Eastern region. The British government, once declared to shun nuclear energy, now has ruled out the option of living without nuclear energy. Germany and Sweden too are now considering the possibility of going nuclear again.

The concerns besieging nuclear energy usage are reasonable as they pose a serious threat to both human security and environmental damage. Once nuclear reactors fulfil their 'working' lives, they cannot be dismantled or shifted. They will have to be left standing where they are, for aeons unknown. Even after their productive life, nuclear reactors actively emit radioactivity into air, water and soil. Apart from the inherent risks in nuclear reactors, there are several hazards to consider. Just think of a war, civil riots, or earthquakes, should they happen, hitting nuclear reactors! The unsavoury effects can be formidable.

There are other nuclear fears too: accident and negligence. Nuclear fears became telling after the 1979 Three Mile Island nuclear reactor radiation which

---

27. ibid
28. ibid

was averted before disaster could strike, and the 1986 Chernobyl nuclear power plant disaster which was not averted resulting in dozens of deaths. Both accidents occurred as a result of management or operational negligence. If those two events were accidental just consider when accidents occur despite awareness of dangers. That was what happened when, in 2002, the Tokyo Electric Power Company in Japan was forced to shut 17 of its nuclear reactors after it failed to accurately report cracks at its nuclear reactors. The company, eventually, was suspected of deliberately falsifying 29 cases of safety repair records.

Exposure to nuclear radiation can cause serious illnesses to people. It can maim people for a long time. It can even affect generations. Once radioactive elements are released there is hardly anything man can do to reduce their radioactivity. Neither chemical reaction nor human intervention can neutralize the intensity of radiation. Neutralization of radiation remains at the mercy of passage of time once radiation is set going. Nuclear power generates waste materials, which can take even up to 100,000 years to become harmless. Hence, nothing can be done about 'nuclear waste' other than 'dumping' it in a safe place. The worry tickling human consciousness is the difficulty in finding a 'safe place'. Dumping nuclear waste in the deepest parts of the ocean, once reckoned to be safe, is no longer an option. Radioactive substances may well sneak into the biological cycle, only to be found, later, in living organisms. As one organism feeds another, the radioactive materials easily ascend their way up the ladder of life to reach man.

America for long has literally dumped its nuclear waste in swimming pools at nuclear plants. The idea of burying nuclear waste in the Yucca mountains in Nevada after showing initial promise has become a bone of contention among those who favour the idea and those opposing it. The current levels of nuclear use by America would require nine more Yuccas this century. Consigning the current 77,000 tons of nuclear waste into the depths of the Yuccas is not the only challenge. There is a growing opposition by Nevadans to bury all of the country's waste in their state as they are gripped by health concerns arising out of dumping nuclear waste in the mountains. The Yucca Mountain—located in a seismically active area of land and lying above an aquifer provides the main source of drinking water for area residents which they fear of becoming nuclear-contaminated. Outside Nevada too, several Americans are not comfortable with the idea of thousands tons of high-level nuclear waste travelling through the rest of the American states in barges, railways, and trucks.[29]

29.Kavin Kanagasabai, *See Above*

For over five decades Britain has been generating loads of nuclear waste without having a clear idea as to what should be done about its disposal. When Britain reprocessed nuclear waste it proved to be a sheer waste of money. And, the latest figure for cleaning up Britain's nuclear waste was estimated around a whopping $130 billion (£70 billion). In the meanwhile, the debate about dumping goes on with no clear solution in sight. By and large, the consensus is for geological storage—that is, depositing the nuclear waste several hundreds of meters deep underground. Geological dumping is considered safe in terms of security, protecting the public and the environment. But it is easier said than done. The exercise may take several decades to complete; technical problems may crop up during construction; or simply, the public may suddenly go berserk should a bad news greet them. Nevertheless, geological storage seems the better option but the politics surrounding it is keeping it on tenterhooks.[30]

Nuclear power plants provided some 16 percent of the world's electricity production in 2003.[31] Power plants normally burn fuel to produce electricity whereas nuclear power plants use the heat generated during nuclear fission by cleaving the molecules of Uranium-235 inside the reactor of a nuclear power plant. Due to the high energy density of nuclear fuel, the total material requirement per unit of electricity generated ... is very small. One tonne of natural uranium generates as much electricity as 15,000 tonnes of coal.[32] Uranium resources are so vast that accounting for unexplored regions can extend the uranium "... resource base to 15.4 million tonnes, which would ensure up to 250 years supply at the 1999 consumption rate of 61,000 tonnes per year."[33]

The advantages of nuclear energy are 1) it enormously reduces global dependency on fossil fuels and 2) it lessens use of coal which contributes abundantly to global warming. In spite of the advantages, current trends do not augur well for a safe and reliable nuclear future though many countries have steadfastly stuck to the prospects of nuclear energy. United States, South Africa and Finland are some of the countries who look at the nuclear option with a fresh pair of eyes. United States not only aims to revive dying nuclear plants but also endorses plans

30.ibid

31.Nuclear Energy Institute, *World Statistics*, http://www.nei.org/ index.asp?catnum=2&catid=352

32.World Nuclear Association, *Indicators measuring nuclear energy's contribution to sustainable development*, August 2002, http://www.world-nuclear.org/ sustdev/indicators.htm

33.ibid

for new nuclear power plants after years of queasiness. The precipitous spurt of enthusiasm for 'going nuclear' in the US administration is due to the after-effects of deregulation of the electricity business.

The market forces have brought efficiency into a sector long marred by bureaucratic sloth and inefficiency. For example, after the near-disaster of the Three Mile Island in 1979, the nuclear plant there has become a symbol of efficiency, safety and profitability. Advocates of nuclear power argue that deregulation of energy will lead to better designs of plants, more cost-effective, stronger safety measures, than what they are at the moment. World Association of Nuclear Operators, for example, cite using a Performance Indicator Program[34] that relates to nuclear plant safety and reliability, plant efficiency and personnel safety, setting challenging goals for improvement, and allowing consistent comparisons of performance with that of other plants throughout the world or the industry as a whole. Even if one should digest the promise of safety and efficiency, from a market-perspective the design of a new nuclear plant remains tagged to a question mark over its cost-efficiency compared to coal and gas. In short, nuclear energy is yet to free itself from the clutches of cagey economics. The capital cost for today's nuclear designs runs at about $2,000 per kW, against about $1,200 per kW for coal and just $500 per kW for a combined-cycle gas plant.[35]

Notwithstanding their gigantic costs involved in the building, maintenance, and waste disposal, even the state-of-the-art nuclear plants remain less competitive vis-à-vis rival energy technologies such as gas and coal. According to one estimate, "a 1,000MW nuclear plant would cost $2 billion and take at least five years to build. A coal plant of that size would cost perhaps $1.2 billion and take three to four years, while a combined-cycle gas plant that size costs about $500m and takes less than two years to get up and running. The bigger the project, the more susceptible it is to delays ... (and) a two-year delay in nuclear projects wipes out 20–25% of the project's value to investors.[36]

The Massachusetts Institute of Technology, in a report published in 2003, revealed that the electricity generated by a nuclear power plant was about 60 percent dearer than the traditional coal or gas plant. Since 2003, the prices of both

34.Nuclear Energy Institute, *Nuclear Statistics, Safety and Regulation*, http://www.nei.org

35. *The Economist*, A renaissance that may not come, 17th May, 2001, http://www.economist.com

36. *The Economist*, The shape of things to come, 7th July, 2005, http://www.economist.com

coal and gas have shot up. Not because they are running out of stock but due to instability rocking the Middle East and its oil prices and Russia's obsession with petty politics with its neighbour, Ukraine. When a price-row between Russia and Ukraine prompted the former to cut off its energy supplies to the latter it inevitably affected Western European countries which were receiving 25 percent of their gas consumption from the Russian company Gazprom, as 80 percent of Russia's gas is piped to Western European consumers through Ukraine. At present, low interest rates in the developed world are attracting investments in giant projects such as building nuclear plants but the whole scenario may well change should the interest rates rise up in the future. Besides, the prices of both gas and coal may well drop in the future making investment in nuclear plants comparatively dearer.[37]

With all the purported benefits of nuclear energy there are still questions that make people squirm in their seats with discomfort. One of the uncomfortable questions, apart from the economic side, is about dumping the nuclear waste. Even after decades of research, talks and arm-twisting no permanent, no totally safe and utterly secure 'waste-disposal' zone has been found. To deposit nuclear waste in a pit and hope that human posterity would someday invent a technology to nullify the radiation is simply a dereliction of responsibility. Nuclear energy, as a stop-gap solution to tackle global warming and as a buffer until renewable sources of energy grow in stature and in use, seems slightly more acceptable than living with it permanently amidst its technical uncertainties, social concerns, political controversy and economic ambiguity. Even then, nuclear power, as an alternative source of energy, remains far from convincing.

The rise of renewable energies

The complexities and the commotion surrounding non-renewable sources of energy and their effects on environment, the possibilities and promises of renewable energy sources replacing oil, coal, gas, and nuclear seem reassuring. With the advance in technology the possibility of future generations predominantly using renewable energies is hard to rule out. Renewable energy is not new to humanity. Throughout history, people have burnt wood for producing energy. Thanks to the discovery of fossil fuels and cost-benefit factors, wood has fallen out of favour.

Today, the deregulation of the energy industry in many countries has opened the doors to bettering their energy output. Renewable fuels may not be the answer to all our energy requirements today but the dawn of realization that we

---

37.Kavin Kanagasabai, *See Above*

may have to switch to renewable sources in the future to meet a great share of our energy needs has paved an alleyway to look at them seriously. Serious amounts of money have started going into renewable energies. Even though the combination of both subsidies and investments make renewable energy sources quite attractive it is hard to rule out the headway that the renewable sources of energy are making into the energy mainstream.

For instance, global wind and solar markets reached $11.8 billion and $11. 2 billion in 2005—up 47 percent and 55 percent, respectively, from a year earlier. The market for biofuels hit $15.7 billion globally in 2005, up more than 15 percent from the previous year.[38] The future for renewables looks bright. According to Clean Edge, a clean technology research and consulting firm, the market for "… Biofuels (global manufacturing and wholesale pricing of ethanol and biodiesel) will grow from $15.7 billion in 2005 to $52.5 billion by 2015. Wind power (new installation capital costs) will expand from $11.8 billion in 2005 to $48.5 billion in 2015. Solar photovoltaics (including modules, system components and installation) will grow from an $11.2 billion industry in 2005 to $51.1 billion 2015. And the fuel cell and distributed hydrogen market will grow from $1.2 billion (primarily for research contracts and demonstration and test units) in 2005 to $15.1 billion by 2015.[39] The Clean Edge report further projects the four clean-energy technologies, biofuels, wind power, solar photovoltaics, and hydrogen market, to grow fourfold from $40 billion in 2005 to $167 billion within the coming decade.

The long lasting convenience of renewable energy is its stock of supplies. Renewable energy makes a country less dependent on foreign energy goods, lessens the demand for foreign currency and ensures less or almost no emission of polluting agents. However, the road to clean energy is not without bumps.

Solar energy

For billions of years, the sun has produced vast amounts of energy. The energy produced by the sun is the solar radiation reaching the earth. Solar light has been used traditionally by households, for example, to dry clothes, but its interest has only developed as prices and availability of conventional energy from fossil fuels have become a matter of concern. The exploitation of direct sunlight probably has the greatest potential of all forms of solar energy for becoming a major source

---

38.Joel Makower et al, *Clean Energy Trends 2006*, March 2006, Clean Edge
39.ibid

of energy in the future. Each year the earth receives from the sun about ten times the energy that is stored in all of its fossil fuel and uranium reserves.

The sun radiates so much energy that it is free and inexhaustible. The energy released by sun provides a viable alternative to the fossil fuels which are the biggest contributors to air and water pollution. Solar energy usually refers to the direct sunlight, which can be used to generate heat, lighting and electricity. Sunlight can be used indirectly in solar thermal systems or directly by using solar cells, also known as photovoltaics.

Solar energy is usually concerned with solar photovoltaics—a solar power technology that uses solar cells to convert sunlight into electric energy. But there is also another important application of solar energy which refers to the harnessing of solar power for practical application from solar heating to solar generation, known as 'solar thermal'. Simply put, solar thermal application gathers solar radiation to heat air or water for domestic, commercial, or industrial purposes. Solar thermal systems collect sunlight through mirrors or lenses and use it to heat a fluid to extremely high temperatures. The fluid heats water to produce steam, which is then used to drive turbines to generate electricity.[40]

Doubtless, the solar cells are still relatively expensive but much of their cost can be reduced if they were mass produced. A way could be found if governments volunteer to purchase solar energy—especially in developing countries which have a huge market for solar energy. Many villages in developing countries do not even have electricity. Exploiting solar energy could present a great opportunity both in reducing pollution as well as meeting the growing demands for energy as the developing countries grow economically.

Already the photovoltaic cells have become efficient both in application and cost. The cheapest photovoltaic cells have become three times as effective since 1978, and prices have dropped by a factor of 50 since the early 1970s. Solar cells are not quite competitive yet, but it is predicted that the price will drop further and it is expected that by 2030 it will drop to 5.1 cents per kWh.[41] The World Bank predicts that the cost of solar energy in sunny areas will eventually—over the long term—become competitive with the cost of energy produced by fossil fuels.[42] Other than its falling costs solar energy also has a distinct advantage over fossil fuels' hidden costs. Solar energy can be more cost-efficient when the costs of

40. John L. Seitz, *Global Issues: An Introduction*, (Malden, Blackwell Publishing, 2002), Second Edition, p. 137
41. Bjørn Lomborg, p. 133
42. John L. Seitz, p. 139

externalities—the costs the public bears because of the pollution and environmental damage contributed by fossil fuels—are taken into account.

With one third of the global population living in villages the importance of bringing solar energy to those parts of the world cannot be emphasized enough so as to meet the long-term and growing energy needs, particularly in areas that are far from cities and established grids, solar cells are already now commercially viable. The remote Indonesian village of Sukatani was changed literally overnight when solar cells were installed in 1989. The equatorial nights, which last 12 hours all year round, previously left little to do. But today, children can do their homework after supper, the village sports a new motorized well pump providing a steady supply of water for better sanitation, and now some of the local *warung* (shops) are open after sunset whilst television sets provide entertainment and a window on the wider world.[43]

Since environmentalism has become such a hot topic these days the emergence of renewables such as solar energy offers some cool options. Solar energy is popular in several countries including America where investors and governments are willing to pay up for the costs. Japan has started integrating solar cells in building materials, letting them become part of roofs and walls. Others have produced watertight thin-film ceramic solar cells to replace typical roofing materials. In Wales, an experimental centre open to visitors has chosen solar cells not only to supply the building with electricity, but also because it can save costs against traditional roofing.[44]

Biomass

We live in the midst of trees and plants as well as the by-products of timber industry, agricultural crops, and garbage. In other words, there is plentiful supply of biomass energy. Biomass is a renewable energy derived from trees, crops and waste. Humans have used biomass energy since they began burning wood to cook food and keep warm.

Wood Biomass energy is released by burning. It can be converted to other forms of energy like methane gas or transportation fuels like ethanol and bio-diesel. Ethanol, for instance, can be used in special types of cars designed for using alcohol fuel in lieu of gasoline, thus reducing our dependence on oil. Millions of generators that create methane gas from animal and human wastes are producing fuel for villages in India and China. Brazil is using the residues from its large

---

43.Bjørn Lomborg, p. 133
44.ibid, p134

sugar-cane production to produce alcohol for fuel for automobiles and is experimenting with growing cassava, a common root crop, for converting into alcohol.[45]

Biomass is recyclable, reusable and renewable. Since plants can be grown over and over again, biomass energy can easily be created. Biomass energy does not contribute to global warming. Plants use and store carbon dioxide (CO_2) while they grow, which is then released when the plant material is burned. Other plants then use the 'released' CO_2 when growing. Albeit biomass blunts the emission of CO_2, the chief contributor to the 'greenhouse effect' and global warming, it is not entirely pollution free as it can give "… rise to a slew of other pollution problems, e.g., suspended particles, sulphur, nickel, cadmium, and lead."[46]

Wind

Man has harnessed the power of wind for a long time. The earliest vertical shaft windmills are reported to have been built in Persia around 7th century BC. Similar windmills were also said to have existed in 13th century China. In Europe, windmills appeared during the Middle Ages. Later, the Dutch improved the design of windmills. The windmill, tireless and faithful, was the key to the successful pumping of fens and polders. It was the windmill that made Holland.[47] Wind power is a reality today. Windmills are used in developing countries to generate power. In the recent years, wind energy has become popular in the United States. By the end of 2004, US wind generating capacity reached 6,740 megawatts (MW) while the State of California alone generated a total of 2,096 MW. The wind-power projects under construction or under negotiation are expected to add at least 5,000 MW of wind capacity in the U.S. over the next five years.

A great potential does exist for further exploitation of wind energy. With technology expected to get better, the output can increase by leaps and bounds. According to the American Wind Energy Association, the world wind capacity, in 2004, was 47,317 MW. Between 1990 and 2002, wind had been the fastest-growing power source worldwide on a percentage basis, with an annual average growth rate exceeding 30 percent.

Wind power plants are widely spread in Europe and the United States with the exception of India whose total wind energy capacity in 2004 was 3,000 MW.

---

45. John L Seitz, p. 137
46. Bjørn Lomborg, p. 134
47. David Landes, *Wealth and Poverty of Nations*, (London, Abacus, 1999), p. 43

The challenge with wind energy is the unsteadiness of the wind. Hence, wind needs to be stored in some capacity when the wind abates. Not all places in the world are sufficiently windy that wind energy can be harnessed. Another cause for concern is the noise generated by the wind turbines when their large blades start twirling. That would give a shot in the arm for the anti-noise pollution lobbies to raise their voice against.

Hydropower

Energy is also produced by harnessing flowing water. It is called hydropower. Hydropower is a clean source of energy. It does not have to burn billions of gallons of oil each year. Nor does it have to burn millions of tonnes of coal each year. It does not cause pollution or emit greenhouse gases. Therefore, there is no need to worry about clearing up waste after harnessing energy from hydropower. Hydropower is an efficient way to generate electricity and can be an important source of energy to meet electricity needs as 'water', its main fuel, is essentially infinite.

The untapped capacity to develop hydropower is monumental in countries in Latin America, Africa and Asia but the predicament is in using the rivers which may be far from the areas of population. As with other sources of energy having a weakness, hydropower is no exception. Regulatory problems stifle the full potential of hydropower from unleashing its energy. There are often legal, environmental and political factors that prevent the development of hydropower.

Problems such as the Narmada Dam Project in India, officially known as Sardar Sarovar Project, involving the construction of hydroelectric dam on the Narmada River in North India ran into a long-running battle. The controversial project was enmeshed in legal wrangling, demonstrations, political debates, media frenzy and fears of displacement of villages as well as environmental damage arising out of building a series of 30 large dams, 135 medium, and 3000 small dams.[48] The project was initially conceived by India's first Prime Minister Jawaharlal Nehru. It took form only in 1979. The end is nowhere in sight yet despite the ruling of the Supreme Court of India to go ahead with the project and to pro-

---

48. The Narmada Dam project is a long running battle between the government whose goal was to construct dams for development purposes to provide large amounts of water and generation of electricity. The villagers of the Narmada Valley feared displacement from their homes, threat to their lives and distrust in the government. For more information on this issue visit the Friends of River Narmada website. http://www.narmada.org/

vide rehabilitation to the affected people in surrounding villages. Problems such as the Narmada Dam Project may be an exception but it makes sense to understand the kind of hitches that can subvert measures aimed to tackle energy issues.

Geothermal energy

Geo means 'earth'. Thermal denotes 'heat'. Geothermal energy is produced from the heat emanating out of the depths of the earth. Geothermal energy has been around since the earth has been in existence. It is produced by radioactivity within the earth's core and by the movement of tectonic plates. It is released naturally by geysers and volcanoes and can be used as a power source for generating electricity.[49]

Geothermal energy is the release of heat from the earth's crust, either as steam or hot water allowing a turbine-generator to produce electricity. Geothermal energy is pollution free. Its impact on the environment is almost negligible as geothermal power stations do not require large spaces of land. Though geothermal energy has the potential to be used for broader energy purposes, finding suitable sites where such energy can be exploited is limited and therefore remains a challenge.

Ocean energy

Energy can be derived from the ocean in four ways:

1. tidal energy utilizes the force of tides to generate power which is similar to hydropower;

2. wave energy makes use of the kinetic energy in the movement of the waves to generate power;

3. OTEC (ocean thermal energy conversion) exploits the differences in temperature between the ocean's surface water and deep water to generate power; and

4. marine current energy operates by using currents in the oceans to drive underwater turbines so as to generate power.

Where there are large tidal ranges either in a bay or in an estuary they could be harnessed to generate tidal energy. **Tidal energy** uses the trapped water to turn

---

49. Philip's Encyclopedia, 2003, p351

turbines as it is released through the tidal barrage in either direction. Tidal energy, while showing promise, appears to have minimal potential as it is still in a relatively developmental stage requiring significant amounts of research as well as money. Generating tidal power involves huge capital cost but has a low running cost. Endowed with less promising returns and a long time lag before seeing any tangible and sizeable returns on investment investors are reluctant to participate in such projects. Governments, perhaps, are willing to invest money in tidal energy projects and can offer subsidies but any project run on such dodgy economics and cagey governmental support cannot sustain itself for a long time.

In contrast to a large volume of tidal water which is then used to drive turbines, **Wave energy** is generated by the movement of devices, either stationary or floating on the ocean surface and affected by wave motion. The energy of waves crashing against the shore is absorbed by an air driven generator and converted to electricity. For countries with large coastlines and rough sea conditions the energy density of breaking waves offers the possibility of generating electricity in utility volumes. Excess power in periods of rough sea could be used to generate renewable hydrogen. There is a possibility that wave energy "… might yield much more energy than tides."[50]

A prototype shore based wave power generator constructed at Port Kembla in Australia was expected to generate up to 500 KW of power as well as to operate in desalination mode to produce fresh water. When the plant was deployed in July 2006 in the open ocean it turned out to be a success. The "… turbine performance was found to be operating at around 80 percent efficiency, while the overall device itself performed at an industry leading efficiency level (independently verified). In general, the device performed better than previous wave tank, wind tunnel, and computer simulation tests had predicted."[51]

Wave energy too is hounded by certain practical difficulties thereby hindering its progress. Much of the energy generated from waves depends on the strength of the waves. Since waves do not surge at constant speed, volume, or force, the amount of energy generated varies—sometimes high, sometimes low and at times it could be nothing. Since the wave energy plants need to be located where the waves are consistently strong they must be able to withstand rough and tough weather conditions and saltwater corrosion. Blindly building prototypes with high material costs may well undermine affordable production of energy.

50.Wave Power, http://www.energybriefing.info/wave_power.htm

51.Energetech, Port Kembla Project News, August 2006: Port Kembla Trial Deployment Results, http://www.energetech.com.au/

With 70 percent of the Earth's surface covered by oceans there is a great potential for collecting solar energy from the oceans. **OTEC**, or Ocean Thermal Energy Conversion, utilizes the temperature gradient that exists between the warm surface water and cold deep water in the oceans since the oceans' layers of water contain different temperatures. OTEC has another advantage. When augmented with DOWA (deep ocean water applications) it can offer opportunities for desalination and aquaculture thereby reducing the cost of power substantially. If the extraction of solar energy from the ocean is done profitably it could, then, provide a solution in generating sizeable amount of electric power.

As with other energy sources which can only be competitive with the help of favourable tax treatment and subsidies OTEC cannot flourish without incentive crutches from governments. Since OTEC systems have not been fully developed, their costs still remain shrouded in uncertainty.

Another type of renewable energy is the **Marine Current energy**, which is generated from marine currents using totally submerged turbines comprising rotor blades and a generator. The energy resource is largely driven by the tides and by thermal and density effects to a lesser extent. With government backing and private investment, marine current energy is considered to have the potential to go a long way.

According to the Carbon Trust, an independent company funded by the UK government, whose role is to help the UK to achieve a low carbon economy by helping business and public sector to reduce carbon emissions, "… marine energy could produce up to 20 percent of the UK's current electricity needs."[52]

Offering a variety of options, renewable energy sources are themselves at various stages of development, some look promising, some still look uncertain about their long-term viability and some look cumbersome and risky from a commercial perspective. In summary, renewable energy sources present a challenge for both governments and private sectors to find a balance between the requirements of energy and the much-needed financial injection that such grand renewable energy projects require.

Still progressing, not quite fast: The promise of renewables

Renewable energies bring a lot of promise, notwithstanding their limited contribution to meet the world's expanding energy demands at present. Nevertheless, with evolving technologies and several energy companies' commitment to invest

---

52. David Hopkins, *Marine energy could provide major boost for UK and Europe*, Edie News Centre, 25th January, 2006, http://www.edie.net

in the exploration of alternative sources of energy there are possibilities for improving and maximizing the potentialities of existing energies.

The signs for developing alternative sources of energy are stronger today than they were a decade previously. Companies such as Shell and British Petroleum (BP) have shown commitment in the long-term tapping of renewable energy resources. Shell has an established position as the world's largest marketer of Biofuels (biofuels are fuels derived from biomass), as well as a leading developer of advanced Biofuels technologies.[53] Similarly, BP is investing in the development of solar-, wind- and hydro-power technologies to meet future energy needs. Mere conservation or shunning of fossil fuels alone do not ensure meeting future energy needs nor will the future energy needs be achieved by eschewing economic growth.

To stymie economic growth on exaggerated fears of the world running out of fuel supply will be nothing short of nursing a fertile ground for creating further poverty in developing countries. Besides, a growth in poverty would encourage the poor to switch back to more felling of trees and burning of coal to fulfil their energy needs consequently adding to even more environmental pollution as well as destruction. This is where the importance of both economic growth and technological progress assume greater relevance. Had technology remained dormant without advancing, the world would have run out of fossil fuels a long time ago.

Due to technological advances, new oil fields were found and more fuels extracted from existing fuel resources. The availability of and improvement in technologies, resource crunch should not be a burden in the long term provided proper research and prudent investment in renewable energy sources are in place. Moreover, latest technologies offer developing countries the opportunity to bypass the same trial and error processes the rich countries of today had to go through to achieve their economic sufficiency. There is a strong possibility to be able to meet future energy needs without compromising on global economic growth provided the right mix of policies and investments are made with a tincture of common sense.

According to International Energy Agency, the annual growth of renewable energy supply had seen an upward trend between 1971 and 2003. Total renewables supply experienced an annual growth of 2.3 percent over the last 33 years,

---

53. Shell, Press Release, *Meeting the energy challenge—Shell's commitment to alternative energy*, 2nd February, 2006. For more information on Shell's commitment to Renewables, visit Shell's website. www.shell.com

marginally higher than the annual growth of TPES[54] (Total Primary Energy Supply) while 'new' renewables such as geothermal, solar, and wind recorded a much higher annual growth of 8 percent.[55] Renewables are the third largest contributor to global electricity production. They accounted for 18 percent of production in 2003, after coal (40 percent) and natural gas (19 percent), but ahead of nuclear (16 percent), and oil (7 percent). Most of the electricity generated from renewables comes from hydro power plants (90 percent) followed by combustible renewables and waste (6 percent).[56]

George Bush admitted that America is "addicted to oil". Sweden, like America, was once an oil addict. Before the oil crisis in the 1970s, Sweden obtained 77 percent of its consumed energy from oil. By 2003, its oil consumption is just 34 percent even though its industrial activity has increased by several notches. It may seem a mystery to see the decline of oil use in the face of growing industrialization but the mystery becomes clear when one sees how with the application of technology energy is extracted from whatever resources are available. That is exactly what Sweden has done, and still is doing. Sweden is utilizing its hydropower, biomass and wind power to meet its energy needs. Technology and willingness of local governments play a pivotal role in tackling environmental pollution effectively and efficiently. For example, in Helsingborg, a coastal city of 120,000, buses run on biogas made from garbage and other organic waste from households and nearby farms.[57] Several such programmes to meet national environmental goals are underway.

Aapua, a northern town in Sweden, saw the opening up of a wind farm. It should supply 40 percent of Aapua's electricity. The old university city of Lund gets 30 percent of its heat from a geothermal plant. And Fjaras, in the southwest, just opened a solar-powered health centre.[58] The efforts made by Sweden may be humble but the results appear promising to make Sweden independent of fossil fuels. In summary, the Swedes' effort is a triangular convergence of government willingness, public commitment to contribute to the country's goal, and certainly the role of technology in making their zeal for cleaner energy real. The Scandinavian air is surely getting cleaner.

54. International Energy Agency, *Renewables in Global Energy Supply—An IEA Fact Sheet*, 2006, www.iea.org
55. ibid
56. ibid
57. *Time*, Cleaner air over Scandinavia, 3rd April, 2006, p49
58. ibid

Enveloped in pollution

When countries geared up for economic growth, they together brought an unwanted bedfellow with them—pollution! Bulging global population wedded with industrialization and urbanization brought the spoliation of the three natural amenities of humanity—air, water and land—through harmful and toxic substances, which we call 'pollutants'. The pollutants indiscriminately and hazardously affect human health while at the same time impairing the environment. The pollutants or polluting agents are either decomposable or non-decomposable. Domestic wastes and sewerages are easily decomposable. Solid wastes that are non-decomposable such as inorganic compounds, metallic oxides, plastic, and radioactive waste probably will take a long time to decompose or remain a permanent blight on the environmental landscape.

In their march towards economic prosperity, factories and homes in the rich countries in Europe, North America as well as Japan, in the nineteenth century and in the early part of the twentieth century, burned coal and wood to meet their energy requirements. A medley of dirty elements, ergo, from particles such as smoke and soot, lead, nitrogen oxides, carbon monoxide to sulphur dioxide contaminated the air. Currently, developing countries have joined the band of investing pollution in the environment as their economies flourish.

Atmospheric pollution by air, though, seems to have been precipitated by human actions during the Industrial Revolution it has, actually, filled the planet for a long time. Global atmospheric pollution dates back to Roman and Greek times—long before the Industrial Revolution—according to scientists who have detected lead fallout in samples of ancient Greenland ice ... covering a time span of nearly 8,000 years.[59] England was no stranger to coal in the thirteenth century. In 1257, the Queen of King Henry III was complaining about the consequences of air quality. By the end of the thirteenth century the air quality was so horrendous that King Edward I "... imposed death penalty for anyone burning (coal). Yet by the reign of Queen Elizabeth (1558–1603) atmospheric pollution was chronic as a result of burning coal (and was to remain until 1956).[60] In the mid-17th century, London wore a mantle of thick and dirty smut all round. 'Everything in the streets ... seemed dark even to blackness,' remarked the Prus-

---

59. *The Independent*, Ice pack reveals Romans' air pollution, 23rd September, 1994

60. World Energy Council, Living in One World, Chapter 5, *The concerns about sustainability*, http://www.worldenergy.org

sian Pastor Moritz. 'This smoke,' commented the French traveller Pierre-Jean Grosley, 'forms a cloud which envelops London like a mantle; a cloud which ... suffers the sun to break out only now and then, which casual appearance procures the Londoners a few of what they call glorious days.' (Georg Christoph) Lichtenberg had to agree, finding himself 'writing by the light of a candle (at half-past ten in the morning).' Even Americans were appalled by foggy days in London town: 'It is difficult to form an idea of the kind of winter days in London,' confessed Louis Simond in 1810; 'the smoke of fossil coals forms an atmosphere, perceivable for many miles.'[61]

In modern times too, London suffered infamous smog in 1952 resulting in the death of 4,000 people in a matter of five days! Britain promptly enacted the Clean Air Act in 1956. On the other side of the Atlantic, the air quality deteriorated so badly in the United States that in the year 1970, it necessitated the "... United States Environmental Protection Agency (EPA) to develop and enforce regulations to protect the general public from exposure to airborne contaminants that are known to be hazardous to human health."[62] The past events of air pollution indicate its presence even before the intensification of industrial activity of humans in the last century, not to mention the present era of much maligned and excessively cursed 'globalization'.

If the pollution generated in the past by our ancestors was largely due to their ignorance of the effects of pollution, and their heavy reliance on wood and coal for fulfilling their energy needs, the current levels of pollution are a combined result of an accumulation of yesteryear pollution together with unavoidable increased industrial and human activities.

Many poor countries today burn coal and wood for their energy requirements. As poverty keeps their governmental coffers and household wallets shrunken, it is beyond their means to switch to cleaner fuels. China, notwithstanding its spectacular economic growth, still consumes huge quantities of coal. Not just China, many households in developing countries in Asia, Americas, and Africa are helplessly exposed to indoor air pollution due to their dependence on coal or biomass fuel. Even in Britain, coal has made a sterling return to meet the country's energy needs. In 2006 coal supplied "... 34 percent of Britain's power, up from 28 per-

---

61.Roy Porter, *London—A Social History*, (London, Penguin, 2000), pp. 120–121

62.Wikipedia, the free encyclopedia, *Clean Air Act (1970)*, http://en.wikipedia.org

cent in 1999"[63] as rising gas price has encouraged power generators to shift from gas-fired stations to coal-fired ones in order to save money.

Of several other pollutants endangering human health, there is also carcinogen, a substance that promotes cancer. According to The World Health Organisation (WHO), more than three billion people worldwide continue to depend on solid fuels, including biomass fuels (wood, dung, straw, agricultural residues) and coal, for their energy needs. Indoor air pollution, according to WHO's Health Report 2002, was responsible for 2.7 percent of the global burden of disease. Exposure to indoor air pollution not only leads adults to chronic obstructive pulmonary disease and lung cancer, it also puts children under five at risk to acute lower respiratory infections. In most societies, it is women who cook and spend time near the fire, and in developing countries they are typically exposed to these very high levels of indoor air pollution for between 3 and 7 hours per day over many years. Young children are often carried on their mother's back during cooking. Consequently, they spend many hours breathing smoke from early infancy.[64]

Water is an important life-sustaining natural resource for the survival of flora, fauna. and humans. A large part of the earth is surrounded by water comprising of oceans, lakes, and rivers. Of all the waters, the lakes and rivers are of greater importance to humans than the oceans. Water, when contaminated, gives rise to a raft of diseases. Poor countries are no strangers to the outbreak of jaundice, dysentery, typhoid, cholera, and gastroenteritis. These are the side-effects of epidemic diseases springing out of water pollution. In urban slums, the dwellers usually drink contaminated water. Nor do they have access to clean water sources. It is common, in poverty-stricken environs, for both human and cattle to share water that streams along the rivers for purposes of washing, drinking and bathing. The River Ganges, one of the holiest rivers in India, is 1,560 miles (2,510 km) long[65] and is an apt example of how human-cattle rendezvous contributed to an unholy pollution. The Ganges once had the reputation of one of the cleanest rivers on earth, but now counts among the filthiest in the world. The (Ganges river) basin has a population of more than 500 million, making it the

---

63. *The Economist*, King Coal redux, 14th October, 2006, p. 35

64. World Health Organization, *Indoor Air Pollution, Pollution and Exposure levels*, http://www.who.int/indoorair/health_impacts/exposure/en/index.html

65. Wikipedia, the free encyclopedia, *Ganges River*, http://en.wikipedia.org/wiki/Ganges_river

most populated river basin in the world.[66] The pollution levels in the river is mightily high that it has contributed to "... 9 to 12 percent of the total disease burden in Uttar Pradesh,"[67] the most populous State in India, according to a study sponsored by the World Bank.

Some 200 million Indians do not have access to safe and clean water. An estimated 90 percent of the country's water sources are polluted with untreated industrial and domestic waste, pesticides and fertilizers, and run-off from fields. According to recent estimates about 1.5 million children under five die each year from water borne diseases. The country also loses over 200 million workdays annually due to these diseases.[68] Health hazards also arise through the consumption of seafood when aquatic creatures swallow contaminants dumped into the water by externalities such as industrial waste varying from mercury, lead, copper, and zinc to metals and their oxides.

Flexibility counts, not rigidity

Environmental pollution causing health problems and its impact on the wellness of the planet is a matter of concern. It has become important on the part of individuals, organisations and countries to take measures to resolve the environmental quandary. Tackling global pollution requires measures taken both at global, national, and regional levels in order to properly utilize, conserve, and recycle existing resources and to reduce misuse, overuse, and abuse of natural resources through environmentally-friendly and economically-progressive policies. Sound measures ensure economic and social development paving the way for enhanced quality of living as well as of life.

Tackling environmental pollution is, of course, a difficult task, but nevertheless, not impossible. It requires collective action, not disconcerting panic. It is easy to formulate laws, but onerous to implement them. It may be less burdensome to draw techniques, but can be more cumbersome to put them into practice. It may sweat less to indulge in populism, but will be demanding to convince vested-interests to forego, for instance, their freebies usually offered in the form

---

66.Wikipedia, *Ganga Basin*, http://en.wikipedia.org/wiki/Ganga_Basin

67.*The Hindu*, Y Mallikarjun, *Pollution levels in Ganga alarming*, 15th September, 2003

68.Anjani Khanna, *Clean Water—A huge prize for India*, Country Report 2— India, People and Water, People and Planet, 31st January, 2001, http://www.peopleandplanet.net

of subsidized water, electricity and polluting substances for farming purposes, agricultural production, or simply to win votes.

The solution to tackling environmental pollution lies not in shutting industries and stopping all economic activity as often demanded by panicking environmentalists and frenzied activists. Such a strategy can only be ineffectual at best and ludicrous at worst. Depriving the poor and developing economies of their economic growth would only push them further into poverty and increased pollution. Dealing with environmental pollution requires formulating suitable laws, more importantly developing the will to implement them and most importantly having the courage to change them as and when necessary.

For a fact, air in many rich countries today is a lot cleaner than what it was just until 40 years ago. As rich countries became wealthier through economic growth, along the way, the quality of air has improved. The enhancement in the air quality is due to three reasons mainly: First, both industries and people in the wake of growing economic prosperity were able to afford, invest and shift to cleaner fossil fuels such as oil and gas, as well as electricity. Secondly, the distancing of large chunks of factories away from residential areas (even though in some developed countries residents live proximally to smoke and soot emitting factories), reduced chances of people inhaling and their exposure to unhealthy 'smoke and soot' and poisonous chemicals spewing out of factory chimneys. Finally, tighter regulations and introduction of taxes upon factories polluting the environment deterred the polluting behaviour of corporations. The first measure was the sustenance of economic growth to reach an affordable standard of living to enable switching to cleaner sources of energy. The second measure was strategic in the sense that residents should stay far from industrial smoke and dust. The final measure was to prevent externalities of pollution created by businesses resulting from their competitive nature to make profits.

There is reason for optimism that countries such as China, India, and Indonesia sustaining nearly half of world's human population and generating oodles of pollution will gear towards cleaner fuels as they become richer. The link between 'wealth' and 'environment' is strong. In the 1930s and 1940s, London was even more polluted than Beijing, New Delhi, and Mexico City are today.[69] It may come as a surprise to see that not just London, but several rich countries, achieved cleaner air through economic growth, not by ensconcing in the chorus of anti-economic growth shibboleths. Studies carried out by the World Bank

---

69. Bjørn Lomborg, p. 175.

have reiterated the fact that while incomes grew the pollution levels significantly dropped.

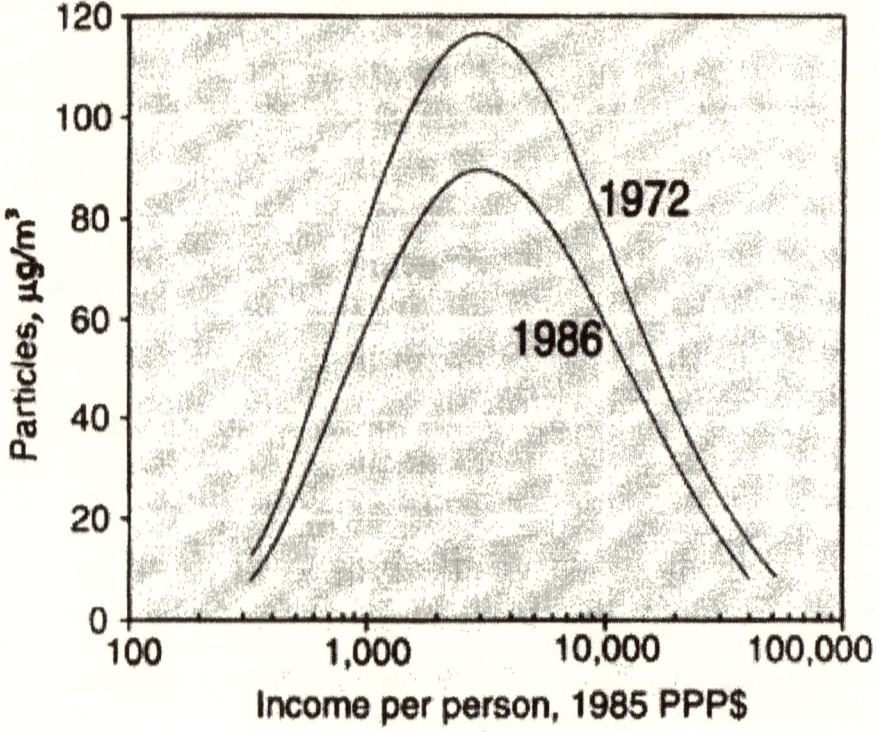

Figure 1: The connection between GDP per capita and particle pollution in 48 cities in 31 countries, 1972 and 1986.

Source: Nemat Shafiq, Economic development and environmental quality: an econometric analysis, Oxford Economic Papers, Vol 46 Supplement Oct, 1994, pp. 757–73. Copyright © 1994 by the Oxford University Press. Reprinted with the permission of Oxford Journals, Oxford University Press.

Figure 1 shows the dramatic drop in level of particle pollution as income levels improved. It can be seen that the levels of particle pollution in 1986 have fallen greatly from what they were in 1972 when people's income levels increased. Similar is the case with Sulphur Dioxide, (See Figure 2) the level of which decreased more sharply than particle pollution as GDP per capita had increased. The trend is common nearly among 50 countries whose pollution levels subsided as they got richer. When developing countries pollute in their scramble for economic development, it is a matter of challenge, not a crisis. What Figures 1 and 2 show is that with the increase in economic growth, the pollution levels tend to drop.

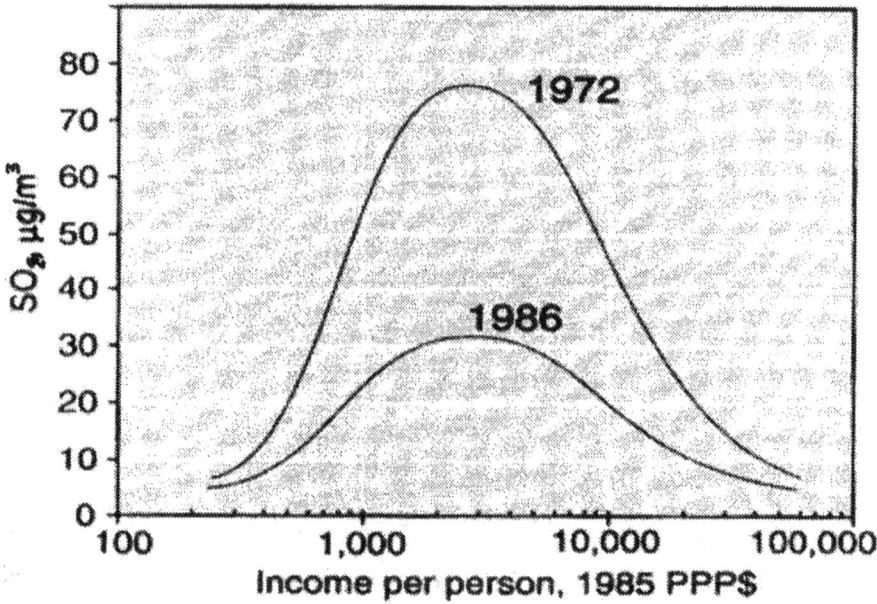

Figure 2: The connection between GDP per capita and SO$_2$ pollution in 47 cities in 31 countries.

Source: **Nemat Shafiq, Economic development and environmental quality: an econometric analysis, Oxford Economic Papers, Vol 46 Supplement Oct, 1994, pp. 757-73. Copyright © 1994 by the Oxford University Press. Reprinted with the permission of Oxford Journals, Oxford University Press.**

However, mere economic growth does not perforce bring forth cleaner environment. It depends on a number of factors. Corporations, even when they do not pay for the environmental pollution that they contribute, stay relatively unharmed by their actions. If they are made to pay for the environmental damage, which they invariably create, through regulations and taxes and introduction of 'bans' wherever possible, instead of letting the ordinary taxpayer and governments pay for the externalities the corporations create, there is every chance of the environment becoming cleaner and less polluting. Markets work better in reducing pollution when corporations come to bear costs of environmental pollution. It leads to efficiency and responsibility.

Repressive, autocratic and dictatorial regimes are particularly notorious for their disregard of cleaner environment. Closed societies have historically proved a lot dirtier because of their immunity and unaccountability to anyone. With the collapse of communist regimes in Eastern Europe and in the Soviet Union in the late 1980s and early 1990s came evidence of startling amounts of pollution in those countries, pollution that had been kept secret for many years so it could not be used to criticize the regimes.[70] It was a startling advertisement for the 'rigidity' of command-and-control style of governance. In democratic countries, the fear of the electorate voting an inefficient government out of power, and the power of the public as well as of the media in castigating a reckless government or activism by non-governmental organisations threatening to dump products of polluting commercial firms, would lead to enactment of laws and regulations to clean up their acts. It is a reflection of 'flexibility' in democratic societies in changing policies through debate and dialogue when existing policies do not work or fall short of expectation.

The fact that democratic societies are able to achieve better environmental standards is reflected in a report by OECD (Organisation for Economic Co-operation and Development) which highlighted the achievements of industrial countries in meeting the demands for clean water, adequate sanitation, and municipal waste disposal. Figure 3 underlines the improvement OECD countries have made in containing emissions of nitrogen oxides, sulphur oxides, particulates, and lead through GDP growth. Air quality in OECD countries is vastly improved; particulate emissions have declined by 60 percent and sulphur oxides by 38 percent. Lead emissions have fallen by 85 percent in North America and by 50 percent in most European cities. Japan, which has spent substantial amounts on pollution abatement, has achieved the largest improvement in air quality.[71] Nevertheless, the OECD report, at the same, has also identified areas where attention is needed. Nitrogen oxides, which are emitted largely by transport sources, have increased by 12 percent since 1970 in the OECD countries (except Japan), reflecting the failure of policies and technology to keep up with increases in transport.[72]

70.John L Seitz, p. 164

71.World Bank, World Development Report 1992, *Development and the Environment*, World Development Indicators, May 1992, p. 40

72.ibid

The practice: GDP and emissions in OECD countries

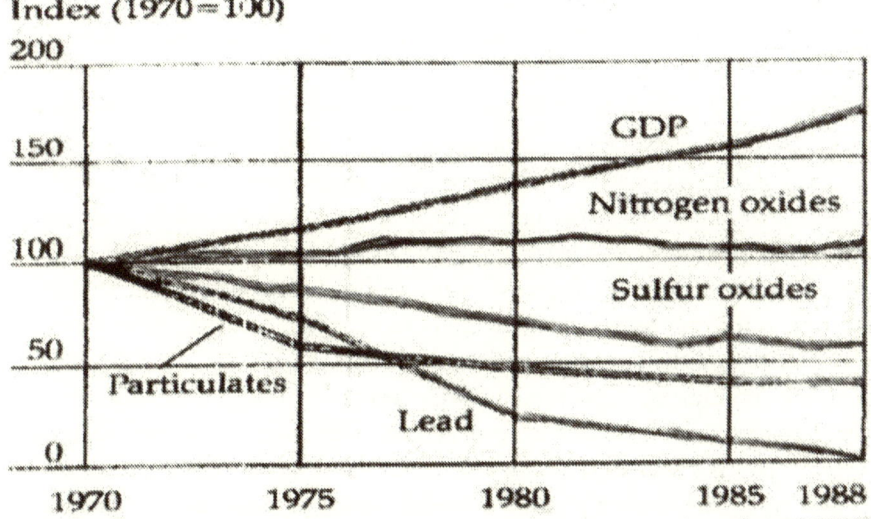

Index (1970 = 100)

Figure 3: World Bank, World Development Report 1992, Development and the Environment, World Development Indicators, May 1992. Reprinted with permission of The World Bank. Copyright © 1992 by TheInternational Bank for Reconstruction and Development/World Bank. Reprinted with the permission of The World Bank.

Note: **GDP, emissions of nitrogen oxides, and emissions of sulphur oxides are OECD averages. Emissions of particulates are estimated from the average for Germany, Italy, Netherlands, United Kingdom, and United States. Lead emissions are for United States.**
Sources: **OECD 1991; U.S. Environmental Protection Agency 1991.**

What is required is not a blind curb on global economic or industrial activity but mutually beneficial policies among governments, corporations, and the public such as the one formulated to deal with the emission of chlorofluorocarbons (CFCs). The control of use of CFCs under the international Montreal Protocol to prevent the depletion of ozone layer has been a spectacular success. Another example was the allowance of tradable right of emission of sulphur dioxide from power plants in the U.S. Wisconsin, in the year 1986, passed a strong state acid rain control law requiring all major electric utility companies to slash sulphur dioxide emissions by 50 percent of 1980 emission levels by 1993. The regulation worked brilliantly. By 1990, overall annual sulphur dioxide emissions from electric utility companies had fallen 46 percent, and in 1992, these companies filed compliance plans indicating that they would easily meet the requirements of the law.[73]

Introduction of effective environmental tax such as the one put in place by the OECD countries by shifting taxes to environmentally polluting chemicals or substances and cutting the disproportionate taxes on labour and capital. In the UK, the landfill tax introduced in 1996 was accompanied with a 0.2 percent reduction in employers' social security contributions.[74] The OECD's researchers conclude that such green taxes actually work. Sweden's experience is telling. In 1991 the country introduced a sulphur tax: this led to a drop in the sulphur content of fuels to 50 percent below legal requirements, and stimulated power plants to invest in abatement technology. Norway's carbon tax, also levied in 1991, lowered emissions from power plants by 21 percent.[75]

Populism is a dangerous obsession, which politicians love to dally with for their petty politicking. Governments are never shy of offering subsidies, ranging from free electricity to water to fertilizers, to their most important sections of society or to any stakeholder that matters politically—especially the farmers when election time beckons for popular political stunts. It shows as much economic nonsense as it represents environmental egregiousness. Politicians know that subsidies are myopic and unsustainable, yet they obsessively stick to them. World leaders would be better off remembering the proverb 'prevention is better than cure'. It is cheaper to 'prevent' environmental degradation now than leaving it to an expensive 'cure' at the eleventh hour.

Global Warming

One of the issues still remaining a thorn in the relationship between countries—both rich and poor, eastern and western—is over deciding the 'cutting' of greenhouse gases (i.e., carbon dioxide (CO_2), methane (CH_4), nitrous oxide (N_2O) and tropospheric ozone (O_3))—the smoky villain responsible for global warming,

73. Wisconsin Department of Natural Resources, Acid Rain in Wisconsin, This information originally appeared in DNR (Department of Natural Resources) Booklet "Acid Rain in Wisconsin", Publication: AM-129–94, http://www.dnr.state.wi.us

74. The OECD Environment Programme, Greening Tax Mixes in OECD Countries: A preliminary assessment

75. *The Economist*, Economic man, cleaner planet, 27th September, 2001, http://www.economist.com

or climate change. Greenhouse gases make the earth warmer by trapping energy in the atmosphere. A warmer earth disturbs rainfall patterns, raises sea level, impacts on the life of plants, animals, and humans drastically effecting changes in climatic conditions. It is not new. Historically, climate changes have been part and parcel of humanity's relationship with the planet.

Over the last few million years, there have been periods when ice ages and warm periods came and went. The Earth is presently in the midst of a warm period which began about 10,000 years ago. Scientists recently have been calling for attention that the Earth is getting unnaturally warmer, since the mid-twentieth century, as a result of increased greenhouse effect due to increased human and industrial activities. There is also a contestable view that 'global warming' is shrouded by a number of uncertainties. The solar variation theory is still alive and kicking. Some researchers, recognizing the warming of the planet, nevertheless argue that the variations in the solar output could also be responsible for climate change. That output is known to vary during the course of the 11-year sunspot cycle, as well as over the longer term, and although such changes have not been matched to temperature changes in the way that rises in the level of greenhouse gases have been, they may still be making a contribution.[76]

Various other theories keep doing the rounds but not limited to that a) the warming is within the gamut of natural variation, b) it could be a consequence of coming out of a 'little ice age' that had lasted somewhere between the mid-15th century and mid-19th century and, c) that the entire study of climate change has been consistently inconsistent since serious study has been conducted only since the middle of the 19th century.

The inconsistency in the study of climate change, however, does not diminish the indisputable sign the palpable changes world's climate seems to be undergoing at the moment. The earth has demonstrably warmed over the last 100 years. The Intergovernmental Panel on Climate Change (IPCC) had stated in its report on Climate Change 2001[77] that human activities have increased the atmospheric concentrations of greenhouse gases and aerosols, recording their highest levels in the 1990s. The report observed that globally it is very likely that the 1990s was the warmest decade, and 1998 the warmest year, in the instrumental record (1861–2000). The instrumental temperature record, a reliable tool, exists only since about

76. *The Economist*, Climatology, Changing science, Science and Technology, 10th December, 2005, p. 92

77. IPCC, *Climate Change 2001: Synthesis Report*, An Assessment of the Intergovernmental Panel on Climate Change.

the second half of nineteenth century. There is also evidence of the warming occurring over the last 50 years that is strongly attributable to human activities. The report highlighted the changes in sea level, snow cover, ice extent, and precipitation which are consistent with a warming climate near the earth's surface.

Active hydrological cycle with more heavy precipitation events and shifts in precipitation; widespread retreat of non-polar glaciers; increases in sea level and ocean-heat content; and decreases in snow cover, sea-ice extent and thickness confirmed the changes. At the same time, the report mentioned the absence of demonstrated changes in overall Antarctic sea-ice extent from the years 1978–2000. That conclusion now is contested by the alarming news of disintegration of Antarctic ice-shelf. The Antarctic ice, consisting roughly about 90 percent of world's ice, which was thought to have been 'slumbering', now has finally 'awakened'.

According to the British Antarctic Survey, the glaciers on the Antarctic Peninsula, which protrudes from the continent to the North, were already known to be retreating and the data show that glaciers within the much larger west Antarctic ice sheet are also starting to disappear.[78] Besides, there are conflicting analyses and insufficient data to assess changes in intensities of tropical and extra-tropical cyclones and severe local storm activity. Changes in regional climate have also affected many hydrological systems and terrestrial and marine ecosystems in many parts of the world due to changes in temperature. The rising socio-economic costs related to weather damage and to regional variations in climate indicate increasing vulnerability to change in climate.

The warming of the climate appears certain despite reservations about climate change whether it is influenced by natural variation or engineered by human activity. A large part of the evidence points to human activity. A tiny component of carbon dioxide as part of our atmosphere helped in the warming of the planet to a level that we cosily enjoy at present but when it reaches an excess the gas can create a great deal of damage. The gas represents just a few hundred parts per million (ppm) in the overall air blanket, but they are powerful parts because they allow sunlight to stream in but prevent much of the heat from radiating back out.[79] In 1850, the global carbon dioxide in atmosphere was roughly 280 ppm; by the mid-1990s, it had increased to approximately 360 ppm.[80] It is high time

---

78. Jenny Hogan, *New Scientist*, Antarctic ice sheet is an 'awakened giant', 2nd February, 2005, http://www.newscientist.com

79. *Time*, The Tipping Point, 3rd April, 2006, p38

80. Aubrey Meyer, *Contraction and Convergence: The Global Solution to Climate Change*, Totnes, Devon: Green Books for the Schumacher Society, 2000, p22

that viable measures were taken to negate global warming but the hurdles in the way of reaching a collective decision are several and fractious.

The Kyoto agreement, a United Nation's initiative, stipulates the signatories to curb emissions of carbon dioxide and other greenhouse gases. Some 141 countries, accounting for 55% of greenhouse gas emissions, have ratified the treaty, which pledges to cut these emissions by 5.2% by 2012.[81] The Kyoto accord, which took place in 1997, has not been an entire success but the fact that it has been ratified by several countries is an achievement in itself. The United States, the world's biggest polluter, declined to accept the treaty on the basis that, India, Brazil, and China, the largest developing countries, were exempt from the treaty at present. Although the United States contains just 4 percent of the global population, it produces almost 25 percent of global carbon dioxide emissions. Russia was recently replaced by China as the second largest emitter, but on a per capita basis it is still far ahead of China.[82] The American excuse, for opposing the treaty, was that it exempts major population centres such as China and India which would cause serious harm to the U.S. economy if the latter placed caps on industrial emission.

Canada, one of the treaty's first signatories, has no clear plan for reaching its target emission cuts. Far from cutting back, its emissions have increased by 20% since 1990. And Japan is also unsure it will be able to meet its legal requirement to slash emissions by 6% from 1990 levels by 2012.[83] If the failure to find a solution to cutting global emissions, with America refusing to sign up while developing countries remain exempt from cutting emissions, the repercussions arising out of such obduracy and unwillingness will be unpleasantly harsh. The International Energy Agency postulates that, during this century, the global average surface temperature is projected to increase by between 1.4 and 5.8°C[84] and "… global emissions look like increasing by 50 percent between now and 2030."[85]

---

81. BBC, *Kyoto Protocol comes into force*, Wednesday 16th February, 2005, http://news.bbc.co.uk

82. Tatyana P. Soubbotina, The World Bank, Beyond Economic Growth, *An Introduction to Sustainable Development*, Second Edition, Second Edition, 2004

83. BBC, *Kyoto Protocol comes into force*

84. International Energy Agency, *Beyond Kyoto, Energy Dynamics and Climate Stabilisation*, 2002, http://www.iea.org

85. *The Economist*, Leaders, Don't despair, 10th December, 2005, p. 13

The richest and the poorest that form a minority population in the world are responsible for much of the global emission. Industrialization brought plumes of polluting smoke with it. Absolute poverty forced the poorest to fell virgin forests and use wood for fuel purposes, thus enabling them to have a share in the manufacture of pollution. Yet, it is the rich countries that consume much of the world's resources and have been gobbling them up for a long time. The poorest, as they live squandering and over-exploiting whatever resources they may have, further contribute to environmental degradation.

Past and present evidence suggests that reducing poverty leads to truncating pollution. Hence, it makes it doubly important to bring welfare to their lives through economic growth. A vigorous economy cannot blossom in an impaired environment. Reaching a certain income will enable the poor to switch to cleaner fuels, to change their habits and lifestyle, and lessen undue pressure on the environment. International experience points to the fact that air quality in most countries tends to deteriorate in the early stages of industrialization and urbanization—a trend many developing countries are going through presently around the world.

The World Bank in a study carried out on sustainable development, called Beyond Economic Growth,[86] underscores the point that as countries become richer their priorities shift—they recognize the value of their natural resources (clean air, safe water, fertile topsoil, abundant forests), enact and enforce laws to protect those resources, and have the money to tackle environmental problems. As a result, air quality and other environmental conditions start to improve. Experts have calculated the average levels of per capita income at which various pollutants peaked for a panel of countries between 1977 and 1988. Smoke, for example, tended to peak in the urban air when a country reached a per capita income of about $6,000, after which this kind of air pollution tended to decrease. For airborne lead, peak concentrations in urban air were registered at considerably lower levels of per capita income—about $1,900. The study further warns against interpreting past observations as comforting and automatic "laws of nature". Economic growth does not, by right or directly, lead to environmental benefits. Economic affluence creates conditions to deal more effectively and efficiently with environmental problems. More importantly, it requires the will and commitment of the governments, nationally and internationally, to get together and decide on a consensual strategy benefiting all of humanity.

---

86. Tatyana P. Soubbotina, *See Above*

The will and commitment is required more so in China and India, who have a combined population of about 2.3 billion and growing, and the possibility of rising greenhouse gas emissions, increasing demand for electricity, and the need for more resources. The developing countries need not have to use the environmentally unfriendly technologies used by today's rich countries in their yesteryears to achieve economic growth. Both China and India have an outmoded electricity management with their plants poorly run and their electricity grids visibly outdated. China uses three times as much energy as the U.S. to produce $1 of economic output ... (pointing to scope) ... for improvement, and saving energy by cutting waste is less expensive than building new coal plants."[87] The relevance of free trade in this context assumes greater significance. Developing nations have a great opportunity to import technologies and practices from rich countries and adapt themselves better through trade, foreign direct investment and international co-operation. A 2003 study by the consulting firm CRA International found that if China and India invested fully in the technology already in use in the U.S., the total carbon savings by 2012 would be comparable to what could be achieved if every country under the Kyoto Protocol actually met its targets.[88]

It is not too late to minimize the opportunity for the unsavoury effects of global warming from magnifying further. It needs courage on the part of world governments to act firmly and the will on the part of corporations to come together in managing the fallout of global warmth. In the U.S., mayors hailing from about 200 cities have committed themselves to meet the "... Kyoto goal of reducing greenhouse-gas emissions in their cities to 1990 levels by 2012. Nine eastern states have established the Regional Greenhouse Gas Initiative for the purpose of developing a cap-and-trade program that would set ceilings on industrial emissions and allow companies that over-perform to sell pollution credits to those that under-perform."[89] To make such a policy work requires political will and commitment. That strategy, based on incentive, worked in bringing emission of sulphur dioxide down and reduced acid rain. It may be a bit too late to reduce the emission of greenhouse gas from going a few notches upwards but once a point of stabilization is reached, it should be easier to steer them back down. Pragmatic economic policies can go a long way in tackling many of the environmental concerns threatening the future of humanity. Conversely, practical assessment of

---

87. *Time*, The Tipping Point
88. ibid
89. ibid, p. 44

environmental dangers can help economic growth to eradicate global poverty thereby promoting environmental care.

It would be erroneous to believe that economy and ecology are incompatible with each other. Although 'economy' and 'ecology' appear contradictory in nature, they can also be complementary. 'Economy' and 'Ecology' after all share the Greek root *'oikos'*, which means *'house'*. If 'economy' is about 'financial housekeeping' then 'ecology' symbolizes 'environmental housekeeping'. Progress largely hinges on both 'economy' and 'ecology' working symbiotically. Without protection of the environment, economic growth cannot be achieved. Without economic growth, environmental care cannot be sustained. Cleaner environment can be achieved not through less economic activity but through acting differently with better use of technology as well as global co-operation.

978-0-595-44341-3
0-595-44341-9

www.ingramcontent.com/pod-product-compliance
Lightning Source LLC
Chambersburg PA
CBHW020423290526
45785CB00002B/707